Made in the USA
San Bernardino, CA
06 May 2017

Now What?/Scott Rodgers -- 1st ed.
ISBN 978-0-9986288-0-6 (paperback)
ISBN 978-0-9986288-1-3 (digital)

Dedicated to the One who gave me this story to tell and to those who lived through it while remaining by my side; Shelly, Ashley, Morgan, and Dylan. I love you.

'And I am certain that God, who began the good work within you, will continue his work until it is finally finished on the day when Christ Jesus returns.'

– PHILIPPIANS 1:6

Contents

INTRODUCTION

'TELL ME YOUR STORY.' That's what I often say when getting to know someone. We all have a story, and that's what makes us unique.

As a pastor, I hear a lot of stories. Those I hear most are of struggle. Life is a challenge. Relationships aren't easy. Work is stressful. After hearing hundreds, perhaps thousands of stories from others, I'm compelled to tell my own. It too is one of struggle, difficulty, and surprise. It's also a discovery of the faithfulness of God. I learned what is necessary to get through a season of difficulty and believe those same necessities are essential for everyone who desires to follow Jesus.

Maybe you're smack dab in the center of your struggle. What I'm about to say can be just what you need to make it through. Perhaps you're new in your faith. 'Now What?' can be a guide to your next steps. And, if you're someone exploring the Christian faith, I consider it a privilege to help you know what life might look like when you begin following Christ.

Where shall we begin?

I know...

CHAPTER ONE

The Beginning Of Things

The Question That Started It All

'WHEN GOD DOES SOMETHING IN YOUR LIFE, does he just do it or do we have anything to do with it?' His eggs are over easy, and mine scrambled. We both have sausage, wheat toast with jelly, and coffee. Sitting in an ordinary mom and pop breakfast stop, drinking diner grade Java; dark, strong, and burnt, it's the kind of place where they walk by every few minutes asking if you want a refill. What isn't ordinary is the question.

The small talk is over as he pulls the pin and drops the question grenade onto the center of the table. Troubled and looking for answers, his hunger for truth cuts through the mumbled voices of early morning breakfast goers, clinking dishes, clanking silverware, and the frequent, 'Want a refill?' He awaits my response to one of the best questions I've ever heard, 'When God does something in your life, does he just do it or do we have anything to do with it?'

Having believed in Christ, he wants to experience a changed life; all the stuff he'd heard is supposed to happen when one follows Jesus. Like many of us, maybe even you, he attends a good church, walks out encouraged, but wonders what to do after the inspiration wears off. He wants to know if God is interested in making a difference in the secret places, those dark, troubling corners of his life that require the intervening power of something greater than what he's able to muster.

In a casual conversation over a so-so breakfast, he's hungry for more than eggs, sausage, and toast. Coveting the power of God in his life and willing to cooperate with him, he doesn't have a clue how to do that in each moment of every day. 'When God does something in your life, does he just do it or do we have anything to do with it?' Little does he know that when he asks that question, I'd just gone through the worst five years of my life. I learned, first hand, the answer to his question. And now, I want to share it with you.

The Beginning Of
Immeasurably More

In February 1991, I gave my life to Jesus. Yeah, it's been a while. No, I won't bore you with old, fossilized stories of bygone times. That's because I want you to continue reading.

There's a verse in the Bible, in Ephesians 3:20 that says, *'Now to him who is able to do immeasurably more than all we ask or imagine, according to his power that is at work within us...'* (NIV) God has done a lot of *'Ephesians 3:20 things'* in my life since the day I chose to follow him, but what I could never have imagined was how he'd go about doing what he did and changing who I am in those five difficult years.

Having survived that season, I now see so many people who are in much the same process with God. Like me at the time, they don't see it, and some don't get through because they abort the process by giving up. Or, they move forward with an impotent faith, believing God has let them down. That's why I hope you're reading this book. Maybe God is trying to get your attention and awaken you to how he's at work in your life even if it seems he's left the building and left you alone to figure it out on your own. Still others of you aren't sure what you believe about God, Jesus, and all that stuff. Please read on. This book is for you too. Who knows, maybe it will change your life. I hope it does.

You see, for years I expected the work of God in my life to align with the American dream; success, increase, prosperity, influence, position, more this, greater that, and bigger everything else in between. In some ways, my life was just that; a healthy, middle-class family, living in middle America with a great job, steady income and a cozy looking future ahead of us. Then, through a course of events, it all came crashing down. It's a scary thing when your world starts falling apart; when what you think is supposed to happen doesn't, and what you never imagined could happen, does.

In some ways, I could see it coming; like a storm brewing on the horizon. What I didn't see was how deeply my faith would be shaken and how low I'd have to go before realizing that God's greatest work in me was happening in the midst of my darkest hour. Not realizing it, in many ways I was using God, or at least trying, to get where I wanted to go. Wanting to achieve and succeed, I worked hard for God. Then, right when I thought all the hard work was paying off, things began disintegrating. Reeling in pain and confusion, I had to get honest with myself and with my Heavenly Father. That's when I cried out, 'Now what? Please help me, God!' Being honest with him led me to an amazing discovery; the answer to the question, 'When God does something in your life, does he just do it or do we have anything to do with it?'

The answer is 'Yes.' Here's how. It all starts by asking a different question.

Answer The Question With A Question

Jesus emphasizes how personal our relationship with him can be when he says in John 10:27, '*My sheep listen to my voice; I know them, and they follow me.*' As appealing and desirable as that is, it begs the question, 'When following Jesus, what's the path he leads me down?' Imagine knowing the answer. No more wandering in confusion while claiming to have a relationship with your Creator, yet having no clue what he wants to do with your life, or how he goes about getting it done. That stops now.

Looking at a few known and lesser-known people in the Bible, let's explore how God's always at work in the life of those who yield to him. You may be surprised at what we see, and that's just the beginning. Observe how God worked in their life, and you'll see how he's working in your life. You're special, but not so special that God won't do what he's always done in the life of those who love him.

I'll also share how this same process has worked itself out in my life. Let me warn you, some of the stories and examples aren't pretty. What I say about life, faith, church, and other things may surprise some of you and disturb a few. My goal isn't to shock or offend, but to tell the truth of what I see in Scripture and what I've experienced as a follower of Christ. I hope you laugh, cry, ponder, and at times, disagree; whatever it takes to embrace more deeply the work of God in your life.

It's important to note what we're not doing. We're not replacing the basics of what the Bible teaches about following Jesus. Bible reading, prayer, worship, and attending church have been and always will be instrumental pieces to our spiritual growth. They're constant in a growing relationship with Christ. In my opinion, they're non-negotiable, and I think Scripture teaches the same. In this conversation, we're standing on their foundation. Speaking of Scripture, let's look at something else that Jesus says.

Freeways, Back Roads, And Bumpy Trails

'You can enter God's Kingdom only through the narrow gate. The highway to hell is broad, and its gate is wide for the many who choose that way. But the gateway to life is very narrow and the road is difficult, and only a few ever find it.' (Matthew 7:13-14)

I've driven through many of America's largest cities during rush hour; Los Angeles, Chicago, San Francisco, Atlanta, Dallas, Washington D.C., Detroit, Phoenix, and Houston, to name a few. Rush hour isn't so bad when traffic is flowing well. The stress mounts when everything stops, and the freeway becomes a parking lot.

I'm sometimes one of the guys who try to get a competitive advantage by changing lanes in the midst of the gridlock. Most of the time, it doesn't work. I'll switch lanes, then the one I just left speeds up and passes me. Switch back and the same thing happens. When my frustration spikes, I start believing that the traffic is creeping along because every other driver's a creep. Don't judge. You do the same thing. Aside from rush hour, the freeway is a beautiful thing; it's smooth, well lit, and clearly marked. It's often the easiest and fastest way to get where we want to go.

When it comes to following Jesus, it seems he prefers the back roads. He leads us off the beaten path, down the bumpy trails where very few are going. The path he leads us down isn't always well lit or clearly marked and can be full of chatter bumps. Losing your sense of direction on the back roads is easy. When the signage is far and few between, you just keep going, hoping you're on the right path while depending on the back road to get you where you need to go.

In Matthew 7:14, Jesus says, *'But the gateway to life is very narrow and the road is difficult, and only a few ever find it.'* I think the narrow gateway is Jesus referring to himself. Scripture is quite clear that the way to God is through his son, Jesus. But what about the difficult road? Maybe the life he has for us, this side of eternity, is harder to experience than we first thought. Receiving Christ as Savior, as powerful as that is, is quite easy. That's because it's a gift from God. But it's the following him that's the harder part, isn't it?

Let's take another look at Matthew 7:13-14 by reading The Message paraphrase, *'Don't look for shortcuts to*

God. The market is flooded with surefire, easygoing for-mulas for a successful life that can be practiced in your spare time. Don't fall for that stuff, even though crowds of people do. The way to life-the way to God!-is vigorous and requires total attention.' (The Message) That sounds like some back roads to me.

My Way Or
The Freeway

I make enough mistakes to create my fair share of trou-ble. But what about the times in life when we're follow-ing hard after God, making God-honoring decisions and we still find ourselves in an unexpected situation, even a painful place? Did we do something wrong? Is God punishing us? Have we gone down the wrong road? It's unlikely.

Perhaps he's taking us onto the back roads, the place that's often lonely, doesn't make sense, and where we're more reliant on him than ever. *'The back roads? Lord, surely not the back roads. They're full of mud pud-dles and mosquitoes. Please don't mess up my squeaky clean wheels, I mean life. I don't want to get stuck out in the middle of nowhere, running out of fuel and left to the ravenous wolves and hungry bears, having to depend only on you. Not the back roads, Jesus. Please!'* Isaiah 55:9 says, *'As the heavens are higher than the earth, so are my ways higher than your ways and my thoughts than your thoughts.'* (NIV) God doesn't have to do things our way. In effect, he often manages to accomplish great things, even immeasurably more than all we ask or imagine, in unconventional ways.

For starters, sometimes the way forward is backward. Allow me to explain.

CHAPTER TWO

On Becoming A Loser

The Call I Wish
I'd Never Answered

IT WAS THE CALL THAT STARTED IT ALL. The day my phone rang was a good day; in fact, it was a good day in the midst of a good life. My wife, Shelly, loved her job, our three kids loved their friends, their school, and their church. I loved our church too; that's where I worked. I loved the team I worked with and the incredible things God was doing all around us. Ambitious, I wanted to change the world. That's when my phone rang.

'Hi Scott, I know we've talked about this before, and you felt the timing wasn't right, but I have some new information I think you'll be interested to hear. Are you available for lunch?' Who could say no to that kind

13

of call? Free food plus some new, juicy details. I respond, 'Where and when?'

Before the waiter can deliver the food to our table, he offers me the opportunity of a lifetime. A day like every other turns into a day like none other as I think, 'This is it, my time has come. I was created for this.' Doing everything I can to contain myself and remain professional, he continues by telling me how much I'll be paid. Now, the only thing I can think is, 'This must be God.' That's something we Christians say when trying to convince ourselves that God is up to something good in our life. Convinced it must be God, the only question I have is the one I keep to myself, 'How am I going to convince Shelly that this is God?' I tell him I need a couple of days to pray about it.

Shelly's not as easily convinced, she's a little hesitant. After much persuasion, I mean conversation, she gives me the green light and two days later I call him back and say, 'Yes, I'll take the job.' I'm on my way to be the big cheese at a big church.

That one word, 'Yes,' would begin the journey that will change my life. Little did I know that I'd be embarking on a season of pain the likes of which I would never have imagined. I'd soon learn that not everyone who loves Jesus tells the whole truth. I would also discover some things about myself that will scare me to death, as well as some things about God that I think will be the death of me. I'm heading to a private prison and will never be the same.

I've Been To
Prison, Twice

My first time in prison, I was a visitor. The second time, I was an inmate. Let's begin with the first time.

Zealous, nervous, and filled with faith, I grab the microphone and look across the room. Staring back at me are about thirty men who love Jesus, or are looking for an excuse to get a break from their cell, maybe both. It's my first time teaching the Bible to a group of people. I'm the preacher for the day. Being the preacher, I believe I'm supposed to say something insightful, but these men are just hoping to hear something helpful.

The title of my first sermon is, 'Remember Lot's Wife!' Based on the words of Jesus in Luke 17:32-33 where he says, *'Remember Lot's wife! Whoever tries to keep their life will lose it, and whoever loses their life will preserve it.'* (NIV) With passion and intensity, I tell the story of Lot and his family in the classic example of hellfire and brimstone, found in Genesis 19, where God is about to bring down the hammer on Sodom and Gomorrah. The sin of the people is so grievous that God's going to wipe them out, but before he does, he gives Lot and his family the chance to get out of town. Toward the end of the story, there's a verse that's a bit strange but sobering. While they're running for the hills, Genesis 19:26 says, *'But Lot's wife looked back, and she became a pillar of salt.'* (NIV) My message to the men in prison that day is to set their face toward Christ, to pursue him and not look back. Little do I know that years later, in a prison of my own, I'd have to do the very same thing.

My second time in prison, I'm an inmate and can't get out. For the next five years, that's where I'd stay. Not physically behind bars, but emotionally behind bars. My prison was on the inside. After saying yes to the dream job because 'This must be God,' everything starts falling apart, including me. 'This must be God,' quickly turns into, 'Maybe I missed God.' That's something else Christians say when trying to make sense of things when they go bad.

The plan, as I understand it, is to transition leadership of the church into my hands, smoothly, over the course of about two years. I quickly learn that not everyone involved commits to the same thing. My definition of integrity is also different than that of a few others. To me, integrity is living out privately what we profess publicly. As flawed as we all are, it's nonnegotiable in my book. Seeing these differences, I start thinking I may have made a mistake. I'd just quit a great job, uprooted and relocated my family, and now I think I might have missed God. The idea of becoming the big cheese in the big church is going south, fast.

I'm not the only one whose thinking I may have made a mistake. Ripping your family out of their world for your pursuits is something I don't recommend. Night after night I find myself sitting on my daughter's bed trying to comfort her while she's sobbing and saying, 'Dad, you missed God. I know him, and I can tell you, Dad, you missed God.'

I don't know what it's like being stabbed in the heart, but that's as close to it as I ever want to be. Like a prophet, she's crying out what my conscience has been questioning all along. Hoping we're both wrong, I say, 'Honey, it's going to be ok, there are just a few things that need to work themselves out.' What I want to say is, 'I know, you're right, and I don't have a clue about what to do. Will you ever be able to forgive me?' In the midst of intense pain and lots of confusion, while sitting at her side, I remember a conversation I had many years before with a man named Kevin, who told me something I refused to believe. Sitting on the bed, I start thinking that he may be right.

'God's Going To Break You.'

I'm in the passenger seat as we're heading east down I-44 from Oklahoma City, Oklahoma, toward Tulsa. Kevin, my boss, is behind the wheel when he says, 'God's going to break you.' Kevin's a truth-teller; he tells it how he sees it, and that day he spots something in me that I couldn't see in myself; I'm full of pride.

He's driving the car, but I'm driving the conversation; telling him how awesome I am. Not directly, but indirectly. Sharing what God has done through my years of service, I tell Kevin about the impact lots of people have experienced through my ministry and leadership.

I truly had been a part of some good things, but Kevin knows God wants to do greater things in me before he does greater things through me. That's when he interjects, 'Scott, I believe God's going to break you.' Thrown off balance by what he says, I think, 'Break me, what's that mean? I've never heard of such a thing. God doesn't break people; he fixes people. He's in the blessing business, not the messing business.' Keeping my thoughts to myself, Kevin remains quiet, letting me twist and turn in awkward silence as I process his statement.

Those words, 'Scott, I believe God's going to break you,' are what haunt me as I sit with my daughter in her anguish. Wondering if this is what being broken looks like, I start searching the Scriptures, and that's when something in the Bible jumps out at me.

Save It, You'll Lose It
Lose It, You'll Find It

I'd read it hundreds of times before, even used it in my first sermon, but this is the first time it hits me like a load of bricks. Matthew 16:24-25 says, *'Then Jesus said to his disciples, 'Whoever wants to be my disciple must deny themselves and take up their cross and follow me. For whoever wants to save their life will lose it, but whoever loses their life for me will find it.''* (NIV) In the midst of my mess, I notice something in this text. More than ever before, I see that following Christ includes the denial of self. I knew this, but there's a difference between knowing and seeing something in the Bible. Knowing is being informed while seeing is being personally convicted by what you know. What I see, and can't deny, is how my years of following Jesus had been laced with my plans and my dreams. God begins using my troubling circumstance as a way of stripping me of my plans, my dreams, and my pride.

Things continue to decline in what seems like a no-win situation, and I consider walking away; letting go of the dream job that's turning into a nightmare. That's when I decide to meet with those who'd hired me to explain where I am and why I'm considering my resignation. Their response is, 'Scott, let's make the decision easier for you. You can leave right now and make an after hours appointment to come in and pack up your stuff.' I'm devastated. In one fell swoop, my dream of being the big cheese at the big church is over.

Trying to hold my chin high because I believe I'm doing the right thing, my heart breaks as I'm overwhelmed with a sense of loss and sadness that's greater than I could ever have imagined. Having first exposed my selfishness, the words of Jesus, '...*but whoever loses their life for me will find it,*' now become my saving grace as I realize I've just flushed my future down the drain. I have no vision beyond this. Every pursuit, every desire, and every goal has just disintegrated. Now that that's all gone, the only thing I can hold onto is my relationship with Christ.

Following Jesus includes loss, and I begin learning this lesson on a whole new level. From the outside looking in, I look like an overnight loser. Only years later do I realize it's one of the best things that's ever happened to me.

The Brief On Grief

Losing a dream job is bad, but it's not the worst thing that can happen. It's nothing like losing a loved one, having a debilitating disease, or any number of worse things that can make life painful. But loss is loss, and it almost always hurts.

Just like the saying, 'Where there's smoke, there's fire,' when there's loss; there's grief. Grief is the experience of sadness or suffering that comes with enduring the unexpected loss of something or someone in our life. Many of us can relate to the grief that accompanies the loss of someone we love. We also grieve when we lose things like a job or a home, or go through a divorce, because what was familiar is no more and what was normal is no longer. Like broken glass in a picture frame, our vision of the future is shattered. What follows is a season of grieving and grief is part of life and a necessary part of healing.

There's also another means of grief that's good. Still painful, it's a grief that's purposeful. I call it 'good grief,' the letting go of something in exchange for more fully following Jesus. What seems like the worst thing that could happen often turns into a time where God does his greatest work in us. *'For whoever wants to save their life will lose it, but whoever loses their life for me will find it.'* When experiencing good grief, it's good to know we're not alone.

The Bible Is
Full Of Losers

Admitting I'm a sinner isn't as bad as looking like a loser. Being a sinner means I'm human. Being a loser means, well, I'm a loser. As a sinner, I qualify for God's grace. As a loser, I want to run and hide, and after losing the dream job, that's what I wanted to do.

Feeling like a failure and behaving as the defeated, that's when it hits me; I'm not alone. The Bible is full of losers. They're everywhere; people like Abraham, Sarah, Joseph, Moses, Job, Rahab, Gideon, David, John the Baptist, Peter, Paul, John the Apostle, and many more who loved God, were greatly used by God, but often looked like a loser to those around them. They were imperfect people, following God's call on their life while losing a great deal along the way, as if it were God's plan from the start.

I'm thankful that God loves losers; those willing to lose whatever stands between them and more of his presence and power in their life. Losing my job felt like a deathblow. I believed things couldn't get any worse, but they did. I'll share more of that later, not for sympathy, but as my attempt to be helpful. When it comes to following Jesus, it's encouraging to know that others have found the path difficult, not just you.

The first thing that many of us lose sight of when the going gets tough is the very thing that's needed to keep us on course. Let's start there.

CHAPTER THREE

God's Purpose Isn't Complicated

The Vacation Bible School Lady

WHEN THE GOING GETS TOUGH; you're off the beaten path and traveling down the bumpy trails, it's good to know you're heading in the right direction.

Do you remember 1991? Not that boy bands dominated the charts or a pound of bacon was less than two dollars, but according to chapter one, that's the year I became a follower of Christ. Before then, I can remember being in church only three times in my life; once for a funeral, once for a wedding, and once when invited by a friend. The time I went with my friend was worse than the funeral. There was a fourth time, but I never went inside the church, we just gathered on the front steps. It was there, on those steps, where something happened that I'd never forget.

She knocks on my door having no idea what she's getting herself into. I'm somewhere around ten years old as she stands outside our front door inviting me to this thing called 'vacation bible school.' I'm curious because no one ever knocks on our door inviting us to anything. I'm also confused because the words 'vacation', and, 'school' are used together to describe the same thing. Then, there's the Bible. The only thing I knew about the Bible is that it's a huge book with a white leather cover and gold-edged pages that my dad has stored in the closet.

About half way through her sales pitch she must notice my lack of interest because that's when she pulls out the big guns and goes straight to the bottom line saying there will be lots of candy. That's all I needed to hear. I'm on my way to bible school vacation, or vacation bible school, or whatever it is. I have no idea what to expect other than the promise of candy being on the menu, and that was enough for me.

The next morning we meet on the steps of the old church that had forever set at the edge of our small, rural neighborhood. It's a tired looking place, complete with a steeple, a bell, and stained glass windows. On Sunday's we'd sometimes see a small group of people gathering there for church, and a few times a year it was used for weddings. I thought it had all the makings of a great spot for a horror film because it's an eerie looking place.

On the first day of vacation bible school, there are about twenty kids from my neighborhood. Being the only adult, the vacation bible school lady has her work cut out for her. She has a full slate of activities for us; crafts, snacks, story time, and the holiest moment of all, candy time.

Everything seems to be going just fine until one of the kids becomes disruptive. Increasingly unruly, disobedient, and distracting, it doesn't take long before he's pushing all her hot buttons. The vacation bible school lady may be full of love, but it's apparent she's lacking in patience. Finally having enough of the nuisance, she kicks him out. God's love may be unconditional but following her rules is non-negotiable. As the rest of the kids are entertained by this unfolding drama, I'm shocked and amazed that on my first day ever at vacation bible school, I get kicked out. That boy is me.

Angry as a hornet, I hop on my bike and ride down the road only a short distance before feeling like something must be done about this injustice. Getting kicked out of school is one thing, but getting kicked out of vacation - with no candy, that's unfathomable. Why did she kick me out? I wasn't doing anything wrong. Well, not enough to get kicked out, I think. Knowing I'd lost my share of the day's candy, I decide to let the vacation bible school lady know who's the boss. After all, this is my neighborhood, not hers.

Pedaling back toward the church, I formulate my plan of attack. About one hundred feet from the church steps, I set my bike down and pick up a handful of

.ones. With little precision, but well within striking range, I start throwing rocks at her and everyone else sitting on the steps of the church. With rocks ricocheting and voices yelling, I deplete my supply of munitions, hop back on my bike, and ride off into the sunset in a blaze of glory. I'd made my point, had the last laugh, and forever established my manliness and quest for world domination. At least that's what I thought. It wasn't until years later that I realized there was more going on that day than I could have imagined, much more.

Before going there let's talk about you.

What In The World Is
God's Purpose For My Life?

Not everyone I know believes in God, but everyone I've met believes in having a purpose for his or her life. For some, that purpose comes from raising their kids, getting a degree, building a career, or making some difference in the world. But what if there's more to it than that? What if all of that isn't it at all, but just an expression of it?

I've spent many hours in coffee shops drinking lots of coffee with folks who keep asking the same question, 'How do I discover God's purpose for my life?' I often wonder if God sends them my way because I've spent so much time asking him the same question or if it's because I've figured it out. Maybe it's both.

Most of the time we ask the question, 'What's God's purpose for my life?' when things aren't going well. Rarely do we ask this question when life is great. That's because when life is great, we tend to think, 'This is it.' But what if living God's purpose for our life has nothing to do with how easy or difficult our circumstances may be?

The average person reads two hundred words a minute. That means most of us can read this chapter in fifteen minutes or less. That also means that fifteen minutes from now you'll never again ask the question, 'What's God's purpose for my life?' Before moving on and pursuing the path Jesus leads you down when following him, it's important to forever settle the question of God's purpose for your life.

No, I'm not a prophet, I don't have a crystal ball, and I most certainly haven't been digging through your recycling bin reading your mail. You do recycle, don't you? The reason I'm confident that you'll have clarity on God's purpose for your life in fifteen minutes, is because I spent years wrestling with this until I finally saw it in Scripture. Now, instead of trying to figure it, I spend my time doing the work of living it out.

I must warn you, in a few minutes you'll no longer have the luxury of being confused, therefore no longer having the excuse of not moving forward with God's purpose for your life. Are you ready for that? OK then, let's go.

The First 90%

Psalm 139:16, 'Your eyes saw my unformed body; all the days ordained for me were written in your book before one of them came to be.' (NIV)

God's purpose for your life is to participate in fulfilling his purposes for the world. That's it! It took me about twenty years of wrestling with the question of purpose before coming to this conclusion. I know, I'm slow. Let's look at it again; God's purpose for your life is to participate in fulfilling his purposes for the world.

The answers to some of life's biggest questions lie within some of the most famous Bible verses. It's as if we're standing so close, we can't tell what it is until we step back a few feet. God's purpose for your life is no exception. In Mark, chapter 12, Jesus responds to a question posed by a religious teacher who asked, 'Of all the commandments, which is the most important?'. His response, *'Love the Lord your God with all your heart and with all your soul and with all your mind and with all your strength. The second is this: 'Love your neighbor as yourself.' There is no commandment greater than these."* (Mark 12:30-31 NIV)

God's purpose for your life is to participate in fulfilling his purposes for the world. It begins with loving him with all your heart and continues by loving people with all your might. In a single statement, Jesus removes the mystery. As anti-climactic as that may sound, it's exciting to know that we can live out his purpose every day, in every situation, and through every interaction. The simplicity may seem insulting, but of all the books we can read, sermons we can hear, seminars to attend, and online surveys we can take, it all comes down to this; loving God with all our heart and loving people with all our might. Doing anything in life while neglecting these means we're out of alignment with God's purpose for our life. Doing these, we can do anything else in life, except sin, and be right on track with God's purpose for our life. But hold on, there's more.

In Matthew 28, Jesus is speaking to his followers, and before his ascension, says, '*All authority in heaven and on earth has been given to me. Therefore go and make disciples of all nations...*' (Matthew 28:18-19 NIV) We also see in 2 Peter 3:9, God's heart is that none would perish and that everyone would come to repentance. That means he wants us to introduce others to him.

We participate in fulfilling God's purposes for the world by loving him with all our heart, loving people with all our might, and introducing others to him. That answers about 90% of the question, 'What's God's purpose for my life?' If that's the case, what about the other 10%? Oh, the troublesome 10%.

The Final 10%

What's the 10%? It's the other important stuff. It's the stuff we're most fixated on and the thing that drives us most crazy. While driving us crazy, it drives us back to the coffee shops desperately asking our friends, 'What's God's purpose for my life?' The 10% consists of answers to questions such as where should I live? Should I go to college? If so, where? Who should I marry? What career am I supposed to choose? Is it time to buy a house? Do I buy a used car or new? Do I continue feeding my unthankful teenager, and when should I quit the job that's driving me crazy? That kind of stuff, the everyday things that make up our daily life.

What's often a pleasant surprise is how much of the 10% falls into place when we live well the 90%. It's amazing how loving God with all our heart, loving people with all our might, and introducing others to him opens up many doors in life. When we major on the majors, many of the minors will fall into place.

For the rest of the 10%, here's what I've found to be a very helpful and biblical approach to making decisions that get us on track and keep us on track with God's purpose for our life.

In all things, make the Kingdom of God a priority. Matthew 6:33 says, '*But seek first his kingdom and his righteousness, and all these things will be given to you as well.*' (NIV) The 'all these things' mentioned here are the essentials of food and clothing, yet it applies to so much more. I use this verse with our kids whenever we discuss their future. Encouraging them that whatever they decide to do with their life, if they make the Kingdom of God a priority, they'll be right in line with God's purpose for them.

With life's direction, follow your passion. Psalm 37:4 is, I think, one of the most misunderstood verses in the Bible, yet it's one of the most important. It says, *'Take delight in the Lord, and he will give you the desires of your heart.'* (NIV) This doesn't mean that if you decide to enjoy Jesus that he'll grant your wishes or make your dreams come true. Jesus isn't a genie. What it does mean is that when you delight in Christ, and he's the center of your life, he places within you his desires. Love Jesus with all your heart and your desires will change, you begin wanting what God wants. His passions become your passion. That's what it means when it says, '...and he will give you the desires of your heart.'

With the details, follow the Spirit's leading. Romans 8:14 teaches, *'For those who are led by the Spirit of God are the children of God.'* (NIV) Pray about the details; which college, what house, which career path, and whether or not to give the panhandler a few bucks. If God prompts you to do it, do it. If he doesn't, fall back on everything else you've just read.

When unsure of what to do, ask, 'Would this decision be a great reflection of my love for God? Is it an appropriate expression of love toward this person? Does it prioritize or advance God's Kingdom? Does it align with my God-honoring passion? Do I sense the Spirit's leading to do this?'

God's purpose for your life is to participate in fulfilling his purposes for the world - to love him with all your heart, to love people with all your might, and to introduce others to him. In all things, make his Kingdom a priority. With life's direction, follow your God-given passion. With the details, follow the Spirit's leading. Love God, love people, and do what you love.

The Vacation Bible School Lady - Part II

While growing up, God wasn't mentioned in our home. Perhaps that's why he decided to send the vacation bible school lady to my door that day. He used someone who wanted to be used by him to reach those who were far from him.

To this day, I don't remember her name. I often wonder if she went home frustrated that afternoon. Maybe she prayed, 'Lord, I don't see the point. These kids don't pay attention. And, I had to kick one out. Did you see how he behaved? He was a hellion. Then, he came back and threw rocks at me! God, I want to make a difference, but surely, this isn't it. What's your purpose for my life?'

Everything she did screams that she was in exactly the right place at the right time, living out God's purpose for her life. God's purpose for her was to participate in fulfilling his purposes for the world. She was doing precisely that, even if she felt like a loser. When I get to heaven, one of my first questions will be, 'Lord, where's the vacation bible school lady? I need to thank her. She's my hero!'

God's Purpose,
A Firm Foundation

Understanding God's purpose for your life is crucial because as it starts to unfold, things may seem to unravel. When things unravel, you start questioning everything. When facing life's challenges, questioning God's purpose for you is not what you want to be spending time on. You have the answer to that, and it's the firm foundation on which you stand when going through the ups and downs. Scripture is clear; God's purpose for you is to participate in fulfilling his purposes for the world. However, that's not always easy. When the going gets tough, you can stay the course. As bumpy as things may get, you'll know you're going in the right direction because you now know God's purpose for your life in every situation.

I now invite you to embark on an odyssey, an exploration of the lives of a few of the people whom God has used to further his purposes in the world. You'll be encouraged to discover that their struggles, trials, setbacks, failures, and even tragedies didn't derail them from God's purpose for their life. The great news is that it's the same for you and me.

We'll begin by first looking at what they all had; that which you and I will need if we're to do the same.

CHAPTER FOUR

Faith, A Smashing Success!

The Last One Picked

FOURTH GRADE WAS ONE OF THE BEST years of my life. I went to school at West Elementary; Mr. Jeltes was my teacher, and we had recess every day after lunch. After gulping down our four food groups - including chocolate milk, we'd be dismissed for recess, and a group of us would grab the football and make a mad dash for the playground.

Playground football to a fourth grader is some of the best life has to offer. It's fast-paced, physical, fun, and full of innocence. The only thing about playground football that isn't always innocent is how they form the teams.

Picking teams in fourth grade can be a cruel process. The best athletes are the first to go, while everyone else hopes they aren't the last one picked. Eventually, there are only two kids left standing. With all eyes on them, they stare at the ground, nervously moving dirt back and forth with their feet. Each hoping they're not the last one picked. Once they select the teams, it's time to play.

The kids run playground football and play by their rules. That means that not only is someone the last one picked, but when they win, they celebrate like a winner, and when they lose, it's no big deal. Tomorrow's recess is coming and, to a fourth grader, it's not winning or losing that makes them sprint to the playground; it's the thrill of competition and the sheer love of the game. Win or lose, 'Let's play!'

I used to think that if I lived life God's way, doing my best to do what Scripture teaches, not only would I be the first one picked, I'd always win. One of my favorite verses is Joshua 1:8, '*Study this Book of instruction continually. Meditate on it day and night so you will be sure to obey everything written in it. Only then will you prosper and succeed in all you do.*' Doing what God says to do does bring better results, most of the time. With so many examples in the Bible of how God desires to bless our life, we can be confident that if we do life his way, success will be part of our story. Maybe that's why it's easy to become confused and frustrated when things don't turn out the way we think they should. After all, didn't God say that if we do life his way that we'd prosper and succeed in all we do?

One day I was sitting across the table from another good friend enjoying a cup of coffee. He was pastoring a church and had done so for many years. He loved Jesus, and even I could see he had sacrificed a lot for the cause of Christ in his community. Sipping on his coffee, he broke the news, 'It's time to shut down the church. We're closing the doors.' I'd known for a while that the church was struggling, but my heart sank when I heard that.

In that moment, what would you say? After all, Jesus has said, '...I will build my church, and all the powers of hell will not conquer it.' (Matthew 16:18) Filled with compassion, I said to him the same thing I now say to others, myself included, 'Thank you for all you've done. You haven't failed. You're a smashing success.' Even though they were closing the doors, for years his church had brought people to Christ and made an impact in their community. That's success in my book.

Every time you step out and do what God asks you to do, you're a smashing success. Regardless of the results, you're a success. That's because Scripture makes it very clear that your faith greatly pleases God. As you live out God's purpose for your life, there will be times when things go great and times when things don't. What matters most to your Heavenly Father is that you trusted him enough to go for it. Positive results might be the goal, but when the results aren't what you hoped for, keep your chin up because it's the step of faith you're most responsible for, not the results. There's something to learn from fourth graders; it's not winning or losing that makes you sprint toward God's purpose for your life, it's the thrill of being used by him and your sheer love for Jesus that keeps you going. Win or lose, 'Let's play!'

Those back roads we spoke of in chapter one are full of people who are going for it but feel they're failing because their efforts don't look like what they expected. Sadly, we live in a success saturated Christian landscape that elevates those who look successful and discards those who seem to have failed while trying. Even when it looks like you're failing and losing, you're winning if you're doing what God told you to do. It's your act of faith that most pleases him, not just the outcome of your work.

The Deception Of Success

Hebrews chapter eleven is often called 'The Hall of Faith.' I see it more as the 'Just Don't Quit' chapter in the Bible. Many are called by name while others aren't, but what they all have in common are these two words, 'by faith.' Due to their unwavering confidence in God, and their undying commitment to living out his purpose for their life, they stayed true to the path God led them down.

It's easy to view this hall of faith as a hall of fame because they're some of the superstars in the Bible. They were role models, guys like Enoch, who was so tight with God, that God took him to heaven before he even died. And there were others like Joseph, Daniel, and Samuel, men full of courage and integrity who triumphed in grave circumstances. However, many of these people weren't the best of the best. Some weren't even great role models. Moses was a murderer. Rahab was a prostitute. Noah drank a few too many. David had his future wife's first husband killed to get him out of the way, and Samson was just a mess.

God used some of them to save the lives of many. Some led a nation or set the stage for great miracles such as passing through the Red Sea. Others he used to make city walls fall, to conquer kingdoms, administer justice, shut the mouths of lions, escape the edge of the sword, and become mighty in battle. That's the stuff of which heroes are made.

The chapter goes on to say that others were tortured and refused to be set free, some were whipped, chained in prisons, died by stoning, were sawed in half and killed with the sword. Still, others lived lives of being destitute, oppressed and mistreated, wandering through deserts or hiding in caves and holes in the ground. That doesn't sound like the stuff heroes are made of, does it?

Then, BAM! Along comes a verse that reveals God's heart for them all. Hebrews 11:39 says, '*These were all commended for their faith...*' (NIV) Winning or losing, succeeding or failing, isn't God's focus. What pleased him was their faith. A few achieved great things in their lifetime, but many of them lost everything. You can try to please a lot of people, but when you actually please God, you're a smashing success. These people lived 'by faith' because they had their sights set on things that only God could give. Ultimately, they had their gaze set on eternity.

They endured in the midst of incredible odds and immense pain and they did it 'by faith.' Imagine having coffee with the prophet Isaiah, who is believed to have been the one sawn in two, or Jeremiah, the prophet, who, after obeying God's call, begins to complain to God by saying, *'I am ridiculed all day long everyone mocks me.'* (Jeremiah 20:7 NIV) If either of these men were to confide in you by asking, 'Have I failed?', how would you respond? Even though the results in their life weren't what they'd expected or hoped for, they were a smashing success solely because they lived 'by faith.'

Which brings us to the question, what is faith?

What Is Faith Anyway?

Faith. We throw that word around a lot. We say things like, 'my faith,' and we identify groups as 'faith-based.' The Bible has much to say about faith. It says the just shall live by faith, that we're saved by grace, through faith, and even that some are healed as a result of their faith. Jesus said, *'Have faith in God.'* (Mark 11:22 NIV) Faith is a big deal.

As important as faith is, we seem to struggle with identifying what it is. Is it simply hoping for the best or believing that things will turn out for the good? What does it mean to have faith in God? And, what about blind faith? Is that an excuse to 'go for it' without exercising due diligence with important decisions?

Faith is anything but blind. It's a powerful and vital element in the life of everyone who desires to know God. Hebrews 11:1 says, '*Faith is the confidence that what we hope for will actually happen; it gives us assurance about things we cannot see.*' It's important this verse stays in context. If not, it would be easy to say that faith is 'believing that what we hope happens, will happen.' As tempting as that definition may be, faith isn't hoping for something better; it's more dependable than that because it's based on who God is and what He's said. It's having an assurance about the things we cannot see such as the existence of God, his mercy and love, and what he's done for us through the crucifixion and resurrection of Jesus Christ. Faith is trusting that God is who he says he is, that he's done what he said he's done and that he'll do what he says he'll do.

Faith Is Trusting and Trying!

Faith takes action. It's doing what God says to do because we trust that he'll come through. It's trusting him enough to try. Based on Hebrews 11, and many other

Scriptures, we realize that living by faith is the same for us all, but the results of living by faith may vary for each of us. Some will experience great success as defined by others, while some may look like they've failed. That doesn't matter because faith is having the courage to do whatever he says and leaving the results to him.

It Takes Faith To
Take A Chance

Returning from our honeymoon, Shelly and I moved into our new home in the inner city of Grand Rapids, MI. It was there that we had become best friends while serving at-risk children who were living in the community. Once married, we went all in by moving in. However, that wasn't the original plan.

Getting married is a big deal and so is buying your first home. We decided to do both at the same time. Planning a wedding while house shopping was the perfect blend for some high-octane stress. The first houses we looked at were in the suburbs, but we had a nagging sense that we should take the next step with these kids in the inner city. Because of that, we stopped looking in the burbs and bought a house in the city, where the kids all lived. We became missionaries to the inner-city. That sounds more romantic than saying we decided to raise our kids in a place where their grandparents feared to visit.

I remember the day we asked our realtor to redirect his search efforts from the suburbs to the inner-city. 'Dear Realtor, we no longer want to buy the house with the big commission check, we're going to purchase one with a much smaller price tag, and, by the way, you may want to wear a bullet-proof vest when scouting out the area.' To say he was shocked and disappointed would be an understatement. Not only did he try and talk us out of it, he pleaded with us, saying we were making a horrible financial decision. Logically, he had a point, but we knew God had called us to reach those kids and we felt that he wanted us to move into their world. We took a risk by taking a chance because we knew that living by faith means we trust God enough to go for it.

In the time that we lived there, we witnessed drug deals, fights, theft, and a drive-by-shooting next door. We had some wonderful neighbors; people with a different life experience than us who showed Shelly and I a way of life that made us better people. What I remember most was how our home was always filled with children. Many of the homes in our neighborhood were volatile and difficult for the kids. A peaceful nights sleep didn't come easy, so there were many afternoons where our house was filled with kids sprawled out on the floor, sleeping peacefully in the only quiet space they could find. Our living room became a sanctuary and a safe haven.

A few of our suburban friends thought we were crazy, and to others, we looked like we'd lost. For us, we did what God told us to do. Was it hard? Yes. Was it a success? Smashing!

Faith Takes The High Road

Living by faith may sometimes look irrational, like buying a house in the inner-city, other times it will seem unimaginative, such as apologizing to your spouse for how you treated them. Whether it's launching out on a noble quest to change the world or doing the harder work of loving your neighbor as yourself, faith trusts, tries, and takes chances.

Faith also stands still and stands firm in the face of adversity without compromising your convictions. Truth can be tough to live, and Scripture is clear on how you're to conduct yourself. It's morals and principles are often unpopular, and your holding to them may be the cause for losing a business deal, losing your job, or even losing a friend. It takes faith to stand for something more than just the moment, especially when it means you'll experience short-term pain. These tend to be the hardest steps of faith because they're often private and go without celebration.

Hebrews twelve, the chapter after the 'Hall Of Faith,' begins with the word, 'Therefore.' Referring to all that's stated in chapter eleven, chapter twelve encourages us by saying, *'Therefore, since we are surrounded by such a huge crowd of witnesses to the life of faith, let us strip off every weight that slows us down, especially the sin that so easily trips us up. And let us run with endurance the race God has set before us. We do this by keeping our eyes on Jesus, the champion who initiates and perfects our faith. Because of the joy awaiting him, he endured the cross, disregarding its shame.'* (Hebrews 12:1-2) It tells us that he 'endured the cross' and 'disregarded its shame' because he had his sights on something and someone greater.

There will be moments when living by faith means you'll have to endure short-term loss and pain, even disregarding a sense of personal shame because you trust that God's way is the best way. You'll be the poster child for 2 Corinthians 5:7, when it says, *'For we live by faith, not by sight'* because your aim is to please the One in whom you've placed your complete trust. You're convinced he'll take care of you as you decide to take the high road, the road of godliness, character, and integrity.

Win Or Lose, You're A Smashing Success When You Live By Faith

'And it is impossible to please God without faith. Anyone who wants to come to him must believe that God exists and that he rewards those who sincerely seek him.' (Hebrews 11:6) The Bible is very clear that there's nothing we can do to earn God's love because it's free. There is, however, something we can do to please Him, and that's to live by faith. God takes pleasure in the faith of

his children. He loves it when we choose to trust him and then try and do something that might give him glory. Living by faith doesn't promise prosperity and promotion in this life, but it does guarantee victory; victory over fear and doubt, shame, regret, purposeless living, and hopelessness. Living by faith positions us for miracles, enables us to defy the odds, turns our weakness into strength, and creates conquerors out of everyday, average people like you and me. Faith carries us through times of pain and loss as we stay focused on Christ. Living by faith may look like losing, according to this world's standards, but according to God's standard, those who live by faith are a smashing success.

Remember our question, 'When following Jesus, what's the path he leads me down?' If ever there was someone who lived by faith, was smack-dab in the middle of God's purpose for their life, yet looked like a loser and who seemed doomed to fail, it's our first person of focus. Allow me to introduce you to Joseph.

CHAPTER FIVE

A Dreamer And A Dungeon

Hindsight Is Twenty-Twenty

WHEN WAS THE LAST TIME YOU went through tough times? The good news and bad news about tough times is that they come and they go. The pessimist might say, 'If you're not going through a tough time right now, don't worry, it's on the way.' The optimist might respond, 'If you're going through a tough time, don't worry, it came to pass.' The reality is that life is full of ups and downs. A great thing about God is, He's at work during both the ups and downs.

'If I'd only known then what I know now.' It would be nice to see the end from the beginning, but we can't. Instead of writing off the tough times as seasons of failure, we may be encouraged to know that not all things bad are bad, in fact, some of them may be for the better. There's a guy in the Bible named Joseph who would agree. Standing on the other side of a tough time, he was able to say, *'You intended to harm me, but God intended it all for good. He brought me to this position so I could save the lives of many people.'* (Genesis 50:20)

God's Chosen One

Joseph is seventeen years old when his story begins in Genesis 37. Going through chapter 50, it's a fascinating journey. The second youngest of twelve brothers, Joseph's his daddy's favorite. He has it made. While his brothers are doing the hard work of tending the family flock, Joseph can be found hanging out gathering gifts from his father, Jacob. He does his chores, but he probably has clean fingernails, soft skin, and prefers playing video games more than going outdoors to fix fence posts. His brothers are also jealous and resentful toward Joseph. One day Jacob gives him a gift that fuels the anger of his brothers toward him. Genesis 37:3-4 says, *'Jacob loved Joseph more than any of his other children because Joseph had been born to him in his old age. So one day Jacob had a special gift made for Joseph—a beautiful robe. But his brothers hated Joseph because their father loved him more than the rest of them. They couldn't say a kind word to him.'*

In addition to his cool, eye-catching robe, Joseph has two things that his brothers don't - the favor of his father and a dream from God. Genesis 37:5-8 says, '*One night Joseph had a dream, and when he told his brothers about it, they hated him more than ever. "Listen to this dream," he said. "We were out in the field, tying up bundles of grain. Suddenly my bundle stood up, and your bundles all gathered around and bowed low before mine!" His brothers responded, "So you think you will be our king, do you? Do you actually think you will reign over us?" And they hated him all the more because of his dreams and the way he talked about them.*' Joseph has a dream of which he can't keep quiet. Someday his family will bow down to him. He's destined to be somebody and can't wait to tell everyone. Likely bullied on a daily basis, he's going to be the boss; his time has come.

Don't we all desire to be the chosen one? Wouldn't you like to prove to your critics that you're awesome and they're wrong? Honestly, I can see why Joseph did what he did. I would have done the same thing when I was seventeen, or twenty-seven, or thirty-seven.

It can be dangerous when God shows us what He wants to do in our life because we have this thing called pride. Maybe that's why Paul wrote in 1 Timothy 3:6, '*An elder must not be a new believer, because he might become proud, and the devil would cause him to fall.*' The Message paraphrase says it this way, '*...lest the position go to his head and the Devil trip him up.*' Joseph receives what we all want, a dream from God, a sense of calling on our life. What he doesn't realize is how little his dream is about him and how much it's about God's plan for his people.

God's Plan For You
Isn't All About You

Looking at Joseph as an example, we see that God's always at work on at least two levels - what he's doing in you, for your benefit, and what he's doing through you, for the benefit of those around you. It's a humbling reminder knowing that there are over seven billion people on the planet and only one God who loves us all. So, it's easy to see that God's purpose for your life will include his purposes for the world. His plan for you is not all about you. With so much need, so much pain, and so many people to help, the possibilities are endless.

Only seventeen years old, Joseph is just beginning to discover his purpose in life; to help save God's people. They're a small band of brothers, a nomadic group wondering through the wilderness, going in and out of rebellion against God. Through this ragtag gang, the Savior of the world would eventually emerge. Thousands of years before that monumental moment, God focuses on protecting them from themselves and saving them from imminent starvation. A famine is on the way, and it's Joseph's time to shine.

What began as a dream ends up being a twenty-year process of God shaping Joseph's character, testing his heart, and positioning him for a significant moment in the history of God's greater purpose. At seventeen, he has the dream. At thirty, he enters into service for Pharaoh; the king of Egypt. When Joseph is thirty-seven years old, the famine hits. Think about that for a moment; God reveals his purposes to Joseph twenty years before it happens.

Don't be surprised when, living out God's purpose of loving him with all your heart, loving people with all your might, and introducing others to him that you'll begin to sense a pull toward a unique contribution to the world. We sometimes call this your 'calling.' As you pursue that calling, the path God leads you down won't always make sense. Kind of like the time I was staring into the face of an angry kid.

God Will Position You Where He Most Needs You

His eyes are aflame with rage. He's only eight years old. I'm twenty-three and scared to death. This night isn't anything like I'd planned or expected. I'm there solely to honor the request of a friend who'd said, 'Scott, you should check out what we're doing with these kids in the inner-city.' Those words would change my life for years to come. Let me begin with how it all began.

Spending my evenings praying and reading my Bible, I'm about a year into my new way of life; being a follower of Jesus. I hate my day job, and I'm hungry to pursue something more satisfying, something that might make a difference. After a long day's work, doing what does nothing for me, I'd go home and dig into God's Word expecting to get some direction for my

What is a follower of Jesus,
What does it mean,
What do we do.

life. It's during this time that I hear about a ministry based out of our church that's reaching out to some hurting people in the inner-city. They're feeding the hungry, helping to clothe the poor, and sharing God's love to those who are too often forgotten. I have zero experience with anything like that, but that doesn't matter, I have a new life and want to share it. This seems like the perfect opportunity to do just that.

Getting involved, I dive in head first and quickly found myself in places that were foreign to me. Feeding the homeless, wandering around under freeway overpasses visiting guys who are sleeping in cardboard boxes, befriending drug dealers on the streets, conversing with prostitutes, and hanging out in high-crime housing projects loving on people and talking about Jesus. Most of the time I'm over my head and have no idea what I'm doing. The only qualifications I have are compassion and a desire to be used by God.

After doing this for almost a year, my friend says those infamous words, 'Scott, you should check out what we're doing with these kids in the inner-city.' Just the thought of being with a bunch of kids isn't very appealing to me at that point in my life, but out of respect for him, reluctantly and with much hesitation, I go for it. Arriving a little late and walking through the door, there I am; standing in an inner-city storefront space with seventy-five kids from the neighborhoods and housing projects of Grand Rapids, Michigan. Having zero experience working with children, I'm not even sure I like kids. I used to be one, and the memories of it aren't pleasant. However, there's something exciting and beautiful going on; they're having fun. Being loved on by some caring adults, they're also hearing about someone named Jesus who cares about them too. They are having a blast and loving it, that is, everyone except Demario.

That night, Demario has been a handful, very unruly and disruptive - kind of like that kid at vacation bible school many years back. Before I could say no, I'm assigned to sit with Demario and somehow keep him quiet. I'm not sure if that's his penalty for bad behavior or God penalizing me for a life of bad behavior. 'If only she could see this,' I imagined the VBS lady would be smiling wide. There we are, sitting across from one another, staring at each other. Not sure what to do or say, I ask, 'Are you ok?' You'd think that was a good thing to say. I don't remember if Demario said anything in response, but I'll never forget his reaction. Out of nowhere, 'BAM!' With a hard-flying right hook, he punches me in the face. With stars floating and jaw throbbing, I'm shocked. Startled and unsure of how to respond, my inner voice screams, 'This kid needs to go and be with Jesus right now. He's going down!' As my jaw is throbbing and my thoughts are to do something that will likely get me locked behind bars, my heart is overwhelmed with compassion. Much to my surprise, I'm instantly full of love for Demario. Simultaneously, I'm full of love not only for Demario, but all the 'Demario's' in our city; kids with a life filled with violence, many who are fatherless, and whose childhood has been taken from them because they have to try and act like adults just to survive.

A few minutes later, my jaw stops throbbing, but I'll feel that punch in the face for the next thirteen years as my heart continues to beat for those kids. In a single moment, I'm consumed with a passion for investing in the lives of these hurting children. A right hook to the jaw was God tapping me on the shoulder. I was blindsided and never saw it coming. God had positioned me right where he wanted me.

From The Pit To The Palace - Just Another Promotion To Serve

Joseph is surprised by more than a punch in the face; he's thrown into a pit. His brothers, having been away for a long time, are grazing their father, Jacob's, flock. Wondering how they're doing, he sends Joseph out to check on them. When he gets there, they're gone. It just so happens that some guy sees Joseph wandering around and asks what he's doing. Telling him that he's looking for his brothers, he tells him which direction they went.

It doesn't take long for Joseph to find them, but his brothers, who see him approaching from a distance, scheme up an idea of how to, once and for all, quiet their loudmouth little brother. They decide that killing him should do the job. However, his oldest brother, Reuben, doesn't think death is the best payback so instead; they throw him into an empty pit. A little while later, along comes a caravan of merchants headed to Egypt, and Joe's bro's decide to sell him to them as a slave, who would then sell him to Potiphar, a guy who worked for Pharaoh, the king of Egypt.

It's easy to think God has changed his plans when everything in life seems to be falling apart. Joseph isn't super human. He's just like you and me. I'd imagine he has to be wondering, 'Where is God in all of this?' Because we have the luxury of knowing the end of the story, we know that God was involved in all of it. We get to see Joseph's story from God's perspective. Sure, God doesn't cause everything that happens, but there are times when he's behind some of what happens. That's because he'll position you where he most needs you.

The truth is that God's positioning of you is often accompanied with pain. But when God positions you for his purposes, the resulting pain can be purposeful. Maybe that's why James 1:2-4 tells us, '*Consider it pure joy, my brothers and sisters, whenever you face trials of many kinds, because you know that the testing of your faith produces perseverance. Let perseverance finish its work so that you may be mature and complete, not lacking anything.*' (NIV) Your path of pain can be your place of preparation.

Remember when Joseph was taunting his brothers with the dream God gave him? Do you think at that point he was ready to lead a nation? Of course not. He had a lot of maturing to do. God was going to give him a big responsibility, but great responsibility requires great character. How is character formed? It's forged. Our character is forged during seasons of pain, struggle, and perseverance. The old saying, 'What doesn't kill you makes you stronger,' can be true. God's using the pain in Joseph's life to prepare him for the palace, where he'll have incredible power and tremendous responsibility.

Throughout his time of preparation, Joseph will experience betrayal, false accusation, imprisonment, and be forgotten, all while he's doing the right thing and living a God-honoring life. When God takes you to a new place, he may bring you down a path you didn't choose, the painful path of preparation. God's reward for godly character may not be immediate, but you can take it to the bank, it's coming.

You May Not Be Destined For The Palace, But You're Destined For Influence

Joseph's story is pretty dramatic. God's chosen teenager survives a horrible thirteen years of the highest of highs and the lowest of lows. He grows up to be a man whom God uses to save a nation; actually two. It's the stuff of which makes a great movie. But what about your life? Does it have to be so grand to be so good? Most of us aren't destined for the palace, but we're all destined for influence. God's purposes for the world include you. He needs you to play a major role in what he's trying to get done. Because of that, he's going to shape you, use some circumstances to forge your character so that when the time comes, you're ready for it. The key is in how you respond to what comes your way.

Wherever you find yourself, remain resilient and respond with faith to get through. When trials come your way, don't look for the way out or a way around what God wants you to walk right through. Knowing that God is using your circumstances to prepare you for what's ahead should encourage you to stay the course. The presence of resistance doesn't mean God is absent. Again, James 1:2 says, '*Consider it pure joy, my brothers, whenever you face trials of many kinds...*' Scripture says you'll face many trials, not run from them. When trials come, God hasn't left you. On the contrary, He tells you to consider it pure joy. You can find joy in your trials because it's then that you know God is as close as ever and doing a work in you that he likely couldn't do if you were simply lounging about in a leisurely life. Standing firm in the face of resistance builds your strength and perseverance, shapes your character, and solidifies your devotion to our Heavenly Father.

Joseph is now in the palace, but he's about to go through his greatest test, the same test you and I cannot afford to fail.

The Final Test -
Forgiveness

The moment has come, and the decision is his. Joseph is standing in front of his brothers, those who had thrown him into a pit and sold him as a slave. Those same brothers are the reason his father, whom he hasn't seen in twenty years, is still grieving his death; only he isn't dead. With the power, and arguably the right, to execute revenge, Joseph passes the ultimate test; he cancels their debt by extending forgiveness. In Genesis 45 the scenario unfolds, *'Joseph said to his brothers, 'I am Joseph! Is my father still living?' But his brothers aren't able to answer him because they're terrified at his presence...I am your brother Joseph, the one you sold into Egypt! And now, do not be distressed and do not be angry with yourselves for selling me here, because it was to save lives that God sent me ahead of you...But God sent me ahead of you to preserve for you a remnant on earth and to save your lives by a great deliverance. So then, it was not you who sent me here, but God...' And he kissed all his brothers and wept over them.'* (Genesis 45:3-15 NIV).

Forgiveness may not be the last thing that stands between you and God's purposes for you, but it sure is one of the biggest things that gets in the way. What Joseph went through is what God used to do the work in him that created the capacity to forgive those who had betrayed him. If Joseph hadn't forgiven them, they would have died of starvation in the desert. That starving family eventually became the nation of Israel, God's people through whom Christ, the Savior of the world, came.

It's vital, critical, and essential that forgiveness of others is a part of our story. It's not easy, but it is easier when we look at things from the perspective of Joseph's story. God can use painful things to accomplish great things.

Realizing that His purpose for us is to participate in fulfilling his purposes for the world, forgiving those who may have hurt us along our path of preparation is not just a good thing to do, it's the only thing to do. In Genesis 50:19-20, Joseph said, *'Don't be afraid. Am I in the place of God? You intended to harm me, but God intended it for good to accomplish what is now being done, the saving of many lives.'* (NIV))

What you're going through may be God getting you to where He wants you. Stay the course!

CHAPTER SIX

He Loved God And Lost It All

NONE OF US ARE IMMUNE to undeserved suffering. What do we do when life takes a radical turn into the darkness; a season so painful, you wouldn't wish it on an enemy? How do we cling to Christ when it seems he's gone and our Christian experience no longer provides the answers we're looking for or the strength we so desperately need? Undeserved suffering comes with unanswered questions. However, in the end, we may get what we didn't deserve, which is something we've never had.

My Full Disclosure

I didn't want to write this chapter. In fact, I did my best to talk myself out of it. At any rate, I feel a sense of responsibility to tackle this topic because many things have compelled me to write this book, and this is one. If at some point, you disagree with my observations or conclusions, I pray that at least you'd become more aware of the reality that there are a lot of people around you, even followers of Christ, who are living in a private hell. They don't talk much about it because they believe they've somehow failed, or that something is terribly wrong with them. Confused, afraid, and even ashamed, they keep their struggles hidden because they believe the reward for honesty may be condemnation. The bottom line; Christian or non-Christian, passionate follower of Jesus or nominal believer, at one time or another, we'll all experience undeserved suffering and will have to live with unanswered questions.

The Bible Stories We Don't Tell To The Kids

When our kids were little, Shelly and I would read them stories from the Bible. They were easy to find because they had their section in the bookstore. Short storybooks, complete with pictures and real thick pages made of cardboard. Reading these to our kids was important to us because we wanted them to hear about God at an early age.

All of the cardboard storybooks that lined the bookshelves in our house focused on the loving and gentler side of God, as well as the faithful obedience of his people. As much as possible, they'd also include a lot of animals in these stories because kids love animals. I have to admit; the animals did increase the warm and fuzzy factor. Who could forget the pictures of all the animals marching into Noah's Ark, or the donkey that Jesus rode into Jerusalem? The warm fuzzies would continue with images such as that of baby Moses floating in a picnic basket down the peaceful Nile river, or Jesus at twelve years old, sitting in the temple teaching the religious leaders of the day.

What Shelly and I didn't tell the kids was the rest of the story. You know, the reason the animals are marching into the Ark is that the people have become so wicked that God's going to kill them all. That might not have bothered the kids as much as telling them that only two of each animal got on the Ark and that the rest were wiped out. We also didn't mention the fact that after the flood, Noah gets so drunk that he disgraces himself by passing out naked and needing his kids to cover him up. We didn't point out that after floating down the lazy lagoon in his cozy basket, Moses would later run for his life and live in hiding after murdering a man. We most certainly didn't tell our kids that the reason Jesus is sitting in the temple talking to the religious leaders is that his parents lost him and left him behind. If the HCPS, Hebrew Child Protective Services, were to find that out, they'd be in a heap of trouble. We just read what the little cardboard books said. Children's books are designed to avoid giving the kids nightmares.

A Biblical story that hasn't made the cut to become a cardboard storybook for children is the book of Job. That's likely because it's about a man who loves God but still experiences unfathomable loss, immense pain, and extraordinary anguish. Or, it may not be a cardboard storybook because kids love to ask 'Why?' And when it comes to Job's experience, there are more questions than answers. Maybe that's why we don't talk much about Job when we grow up, because, as adults, we still ask 'Why?' We don't question why we shouldn't stick our finger in the light socket, or run across the street without looking both ways, but we ask why do bad things happen to good people. If God is love, then why is there so much pain in the world? If he doesn't cause it, why does he allow it? And the list goes on.

When it comes to living God's purpose for our life and going down the path Jesus leads, this topic, I feel, must be addressed.

'God Is Good, All The Time.'

I used to work at a church that would often say, 'God is good, all the time.' I remember thinking it to be quite a cliché, and I'm not a big fan of cliché's, especially those of the Christian sort. Over time, however, I realized that the issue wasn't with the phrase as much as it was with me, and my dislike for clichés, so I just had to get over it. Eventually, I'd join in and say it with sincere passion.

I never questioned the truth of the statement, 'God is good, all the time,' until I went through my personal prison experience mentioned in chapter two. It was then that I began to doubt the goodness of God. Without a basic understanding of Scripture, it can be easy to doubt that God is good. Because of that, let's take a quick look at some of the sources of pain and suffering that can come our way.

The Bible is quite clear that God is good, even though bad things still happen. Jesus taught that both good and evil do exist in this world when he said in John 10:10, *'The thief's purpose is to steal and kill and destroy. My purpose is to give them a rich and satisfying life.'* When teaching the meaning of this verse to kids, I say, 'God is good, and the devil is bad.' That's not deep theology, but it's true theology. God wants to do good things in our lives, and even though the devil isn't behind every bad thing in the world, he is behind some of it.

We also see something revealing in Romans 5:12, *'When Adam sinned, sin entered the world. Adam's sin brought death, so death spread to everyone, for everyone sinned.'* We see here that death, as well as the origin of sickness, is the result of sin. Bad things happen because we live in a broken world.

If that's not enough, we have the issue of free will. How did Adam sin? By disobeying the only thing God told him not to do; to eat from the tree of the knowledge of good and evil - Genesis 2:16-17. God gave him a choice and that ability to choose still stands. Sometimes we choose wrong and pay the price. Sometimes someone else chooses wrong and we pay the price. Intentional or not, there are consequences to our choices. Sickness, disease, racism, car crashes, and other horrible things can be the result of Adam's original sin, our sin, pride, bad decisions, or just falling asleep at the wheel.

But what about the times when bad things happen for no apparent reason? If God is good and we're living right, what do we do when something horrible still happens? How do we respond to undeserved suffering? That's what happened to Job. Thankfully, God shows us why Job went through what he went through, but what God didn't do was let Job in on it. When it comes to living through undeserved suffering, Job has a lot to teach us. Before he does, I'll let you in on the time when I began to doubt the goodness of God.

Going Public With A Private Pain

These are a few journal entries from a time when I doubted the goodness of God.

Journal Entry - December 12, 'I'm done. I blew it. I'm spent. I made directional decisions that have cost my family incomprehensible pain. I'm sorry. I'm finished with serving the church...'

Journal Entry - December 26, (Two weeks later, the day after Christmas) 'I'm sorrier than words can express. I apologize to everyone. I thought my intent was for good. I guess that trying to make a difference has cost me nearly everything. I have no joy. I live in constant emotional pain. Jesus, please help me.'

Journal Entry - November 10, (Eleven months later) 'God, if I'm sick, please heal me. If I'm a horrible leader, please remove me. If Satan has oppressed me, please deliver me. Jesus, Jesus, Jesus, I never want to experience another day or week like I've just had...EVER.'

After losing the dream job of being the big cheese at the big church, I'd become a free agent in the church leadership market. Churches are always looking for leaders who can make things happen. Because my experience outweighed my weaknesses, I was marketable. I quickly had some job opportunities come my way. Broken from what I'd just gone through, I was hungry to put things behind me and jump into something new. Looking back, that was a mistake. Whenever we go through a traumatic experience, it's best to give ourselves some time to heal, let the fog clear, and to recalibrate before moving forward with big decisions. I didn't do that.

Not long after, I'm sitting on an airplane writing down a 'pro's and con's' list of the opportunities I'm considering. One particular job had more pro's than the others, so I leaned into that opportunity and eventually got the job.

I'm on the job for less than a month, and I know I've made a mistake. Even though I'm meeting a lot of wonderful people, excited about the future, and already doing well in my role, it's still evident to me that I've made a mistake. I should never have taken the job. Overlooking a bunch of important factors to my wife and me, I was hurting so much during the interview process that I wasn't thinking straight. Having uprooted my family again to take a new job I knew was destined to fail, I became desperate.

One night I'm so overwhelmed that I go into the bedroom, close the door and sit on the floor. Leaning against the bed while clinching a towel between my teeth to mute my cry, I sob in despair. I wonder if the best thing to do is to end it all. It's the scariest moment of my life. Instantly, my mind floods with images of my family. Shelly, who'd stuck with me through thick and thin. Our kids, who are beautiful, bold, and strong - their whole life ahead of them. As quickly as the thought to end it all comes, I realize I've gone beyond my ability to pick myself up. I need help, and I need it fast. I commit to lean into God for strength and lean on some close friends for support.

Although I knew I'd made a mistake and I was going crazy on the inside, God is still working through me. The things I'm leading are growing and going strong, and our family is doing well. Still feeling like I have nowhere to turn, I keep on keeping on, but I can't shake the waves of hopelessness.

Ten, twelve, fifteen times a day, or more, I'm blind-sided with an overwhelming sense of hopelessness. It lasts anywhere from a few minutes to an hour, and sometimes, the rest of the day. I can't control it, and it's controlling me.

Trying to figure out where these waves of hopelessness are coming from, I began researching it online. After typing in phrases such as, 'Why do I feel hopeless?', it doesn't take long to see a pattern emerge. The word 'depression' keeps coming up. 'Me? Depressed? No way! I'm stronger than that; this can't be. I'm a leader in the church. Things are growing around me. God is using me to change lives.' With that and more rolling around in my mind, I take a few online tests and the results kept coming back saying that I am moderately depressed. Reading about the details of moderate depression, I see that 'moderate' means that the treatment doesn't necessarily need to include medicine. That's a relief because I feel it's easier to keep my little secret a secret if I don't have to hide a bottle of prescription meds.

I'm embarrassed and ashamed, not because I'm experiencing a moderate level of depression; I have many friends who wrestle with depression. I'm ashamed that I can't fix this on my own. Adding to my struggles, the nature of my job; the one I know I shouldn't be doing, is an endless amount of work. I feel like an injured soldier, waiting for a medic, but none comes, and I can't escape the battlefield. During this painful time, I learn how to walk closer to Christ.

desperation, I regularly get on my knees, plant my face in the carpet and cry out to God for strength. Sometimes I get in my car and just drive around yelling, cussing, and weeping as I call out to God. I know I'm the one who made the decision to put my family in the situation we are in, and I feel horrible for it. I am also angry at God for not intervening. I feel I've lived a life of honesty and integrity while sacrificially serving others for years and years. I feel like my suffering is undeserved and that God no longer cares about my family or me. Ultimately, with Shelly's agreement, I do what's best for my family and my sanity, I quit my job.

There I stand, not knowing what's next, where to go, or how we're going to survive financially. As angry as I am at God and as disappointed as I am with myself, I know there's nowhere to go but closer to Christ. Confident that the one thing that can bring me through anything is to sit at the feet of Jesus, I begin to experience the power and presence of God in a way that sustains me, one hour at a time, one day at a time.

In many ways, my situation wasn't anything like what Job went through. He lost his family, his health, and his wealth. I didn't lose my family, my health was alright, and I had only very little wealth to lose. Similar to Job, I learned that it's better to know God than to know why. I had to live through my suffering while God chose to remain silent in response to my questions. I learned that God doesn't always deliver us from our suffering, but he does give us the strength to walk through it.

Job, God, And Satan

Job is an upright and wealthy family man. Job 1:1-2 says, *'There once was a man named Job who lived in the land of Uz. He was blameless-a man of complete integrity. He feared God and stayed away from evil. He had seven sons and three daughters.'* The next verse says, *'He was, in fact, the richest person in that entire area.'* The Bible then describes some sort of heavenly tribunal taking place. In verse six we read, *'One day the members of the heavenly court came to present themselves before the Lord, and the Accuser, Satan, came with them.'* God asks Satan where he'd come from and he says, *'From roaming through the earth and going back and forth in it.'* (Job 1:7) God responds, *'Have you considered my servant Job? There is no one on earth like him; he is blameless and upright, a man who fears God and shuns evil.'* (Job 1:8) Satan then challenges God's affirmation of Job by accusing Job of having a hidden agenda. He suggests that Job worships God only because of what he can get from him. Satan believes that if God removes his blessing from Job's life, that he'll abandon his faith and curse God to his face. He's basically saying, 'Job doesn't love you, he only loves what you do for him.' So God takes him up on his offer and gives Satan permission to wreak havoc on everything in Job's life. The only thing that's off limits is killing Job. I wonder if that's because God needs Job to live through his suffering so that he can prove to Satan how wrong he is. If Satan kills Job, they'll never know.

For centuries this story has created confusion and controversy. Why would God allow such cruel and unusual punishment to happen in Job's life? Someone completely innocent even? God knows what he's doing, and, as we'll soon see, Job's life is restored and God is glorified through it. As difficult to understand as this story may be, there's a lot we can learn from Job when it comes to walking through our season of suffering.

Job, His Wife, Some Friends, And The Harmful Half-Truth

After killing Job's children and destroying all that he owns, Satan has permission to torture him with terrible boils from the top of his head to the bottom of his feet. Of all that we want from life, relief from pain is near the top of the list.

Grieving herself, and seeing Job's anguish, his wife says to him, '*Are you still trying to maintain your integrity? Curse God and die.' But Job replies, 'You talk like a foolish woman. Should we accept only good things from the hand of God and never anything bad?' So in all this, Job said nothing wrong.'* (Job 2:9-10)

Hearing of his tragedy and suffering, Job's friends come to try and console him. Approaching him, they can hardly recognize him because he's such a mess. Together they wail, tear their clothes, throw dust in the air, and grieve with their friend. His suffering is so great that, aside from weeping and wailing, they're speechless for the first seven days of sitting with him. Chapter 2:13 says, *'No one said a word to Job, for they saw that his suffering was too great for words.'* Silence from a friend who is present in your pain is often better than a friend trying to explain why you're there in the first place.

After seven days of sitting in silence, Job's friends can't hold back any longer; they feel they have to say something. They begin with the classic response that bad things don't happen to good people. There must be a reason for this. Perhaps there's a secret sin in his life, or he doesn't have enough faith, or he isn't reading his Bible enough, or his trust in God is lacking. Job's friends believe in cause and effect; do good and good things happen, do bad and bad things happen, virtue is always rewarded, and vice is always punished. These are only half-truths because Job's friends don't believe in undeserved suffering. They think they have all the answers to the question, 'Why?' The problem with friends like this is that there's always some truth in what they say. But it's also mixed with falsehood. Truth mixed with untruth is a dangerous cocktail. While they're still pontificating on why this and why that, Job reaches a boiling point and says, *'How long will you torture me? How long will you try to crush me with your words?'* (Job 19:1) Confident he's done nothing wrong to deserve this, he says, *'But as for me, I know that my Redeemer lives, and he will stand upon the earth at last.'*

(Job 19:25) He believes that, in the end, God will stand up for him, that righteousness and justice will prevail.

In the meantime, he's human, so he struggles. With great frustration, he demands justice. After saying all he had to say, and after his friend Elihu's long speech, God finally answers Job. In chapter 38:3, God says, '*Brace yourself like a man, because I have some questions for you, and you must answer them.*' He asks who's the sovereign and all-powerful one here, you or me? With repentance, Job responds, '*I had only heard about you before, but now I have seen you with my own eyes. I take back everything I said, and I sit in dust and ashes to show my repentance.*' (Job 42:5-7)

Soon after, God restores his fortunes by giving him twice as much as he had before. Chapter 42:12 says, '*So the Lord blessed Job in the second half of his life even more than in the beginning.*'

Job Isn't The Norm, But Living With Unanswered Questions Is

Job loved God and lost it all. Through his suffering, anger, confusion, and even some misdirected council from his friends, he chose to hold firmly to his faith that God is good. God reserves the right to remain silent. He never promised he'd answer all our questions. There will come a day when everything makes sense, but that likely won't happen until we step into eternity. Let's not live our life in a bitter reaction to God's silence, let's live based on where he's loud and clear. His love is constant, he's always at work in us and around us, and we can trust him. You can trust him. When life deals you loss, know that his love never fails. As hard is it can be, let's not let the unanswered questions drive us crazy, let's use them as the fuel that drives us closer to God.

I'm the billboard for imperfect people. I'm also living proof that, when walking through a season of darkness, God is faithful. I certainly didn't go through what Job went through, and I may not have gone through what you're going through, but I made it through and I've experienced God's healing and renewal. Being on the other side, I'm now able to see my season of suffering as a gift. In those moments of screaming at God while he was silent, begging him to step in and change my circumstance, what I didn't see was how he was changing me. Was God the author of all my suffering? No. Did he do something beautiful in the midst of my suffering? Yes. I now know what it means to have joy, to experience peace, and to live with contentment. Will he do the same for you? Absolutely.

James 5:10-11 says, *'For examples of patience in suffering, dear brothers and sisters, look at the prophets who spoke in the name of the Lord. We give great honor to those who endure under suffering. For instance, you know about Job, a man of great endurance. You can see how the Lord was kind to him at the end, for the Lord is full of tenderness and mercy.'*

God is good, all the time.

CHAPTER SEVEN

When Doing Right Goes Wrong

Doing The Right Thing Was A New Thing

WE TEND TO REMEMBER WHERE WE WERE when something significant happened in our life. Soon after becoming a Christian, I was working in a restaurant. It was a big place with two large dining rooms, three banquet areas, and a bowling alley with all the cool stuff like pool tables, video games, bowling balls, ugly shoes, nachos, and beer. I learned how to cook while working in that restaurant. I also discovered how God takes possession of our conscience when we give Him control of our life.

One day I'm cleaning up a banquet room after cooking for a group of about twenty people who'd gathered for a lunch meeting. In another room, next to the one I'm cleaning, are two older men sitting at a small table playing cards and drinking scotch. One of them is the owner of the restaurant. As a young man, I'm intimidated by the owner. He isn't a bad guy; in fact, he's very kind and caring. However, it's his title that makes me nervous and insecure whenever he's around.

While cleaning up the room, I drop a small glass table topper, and it smashes into pieces. I immediately find myself standing at a crossroads. What should I do? My first thought is to throw the chunks of broken glass in the trash and not say a thing. That's what I'd done before in similar situations; keep quiet, cover it up, and move on. But now that I have Jesus in my life, things are different, I'm different. The shattered table topper evokes a voice in my conscience that says, 'You can't hide this. You need to tell the owner what you've done.'

My heart racing, I pick up the pieces, walk into the next room, interrupt the card game and hold out my hand, full of broken glass. I tell the owner what happened and that it's my fault. Expecting disappointment and a verbal dress-down, he says something to me that I've never forgotten. 'Scott, everyone makes mistakes, but when you're willing to admit your mistakes, you start becoming a man.'

God used a man who cared more about me than he did a silly table topper to teach me a life lesson about honesty and character. That was a big deal because most of my life I'd had no problem hiding the truth. In fact, I was a good liar and never felt it was wrong because lying helped to keep me out of trouble. Things changed when I began following Christ. My conscience became sensitive to telling the truth. What was once easy, even natural, lying became awkward and uncomfortable. I didn't realize it then, but I'd later understand why this change had taken place. In John 14:6, Jesus says, *'I am the way, the truth, and the life.'* Referring to the devil in John 8:44, he also says, *'He has always hated the truth, because there is no truth in him. When he lies, it is consistent with his character; for he is a liar and the father of lies.'* I was taking on the character of Christ and shedding that of the one who loves to lie. I did what was right by telling the truth and was rewarded for it with a great life lesson. But things don't always go that way.

What do you do when you do what God tells you to do, and it goes wrong? What do you do when you're penalized and even punished for doing the right thing, the very thing God wants you to do?

God Is Good, Heads Still Roll

John the Baptist is someone who's sold out, a radical for Jesus, a prophet sent by God to prepare the way for the Messiah. Filled with the Spirit, he's a kingdom-shaker and a world-changer. Polarizing and disruptive, John does what prophets do; they shake things up.

A preacher with a clear message, 'Repent!', John is set apart from birth for God's purpose of preparing the way for the coming Messiah. People flock to hear him even though he doesn't have a website, email list, or social media campaign. They travel to the edge of town to hear him talk about turning away from sin and turning to God. Matthew 3:1-2 says, *'In those days John the Baptist came to the Judean wilderness and began preaching. His message was, 'Repent of your sins and turn to God, for the Kingdom of Heaven is near.''* Speaking with authority, his message is irresistible - being right with God is something we all desire. He challenges his audience to take action on what they hear and go public with their commitment to repent and turn to God by getting baptized in the river.

John doesn't hold back with the religious leaders who come to see what's going on. His message to them is the same as it is to everyone else; *'But when he saw many Pharisees and Sadducees coming to watch him baptize, he denounced them. "You brood of snakes!" he exclaimed. "Who warned you to flee God's coming wrath? Prove by the way you live that you have repented of your sins and turned to God."'* (Matthew 3:7-8)

Doing what God had called him to do, John is fulfilling God's purpose for his life. He's in the zone; his ministry is growing and impacting people's lives. He even baptizes Jesus, who would later say, *'I tell you the truth, of all who have ever lived, none is greater than John the Baptist.'* (Matthew 11:11) His life is, in many ways, one that most of us would envy. A storybook tale of risk-taking and faith, obedience and commitment, impact and provision. That is, until a guy named Herod comes along.

Politics and Religion Anyone?

Herod is a politician and a people pleaser who respects John and considers him a good man. He enjoys listening to him, even though he doesn't always understand him. Having a habit of telling the truth, John calls Herod out about taking his brother's wife, Herodias, to be his own and pointing out that it's immoral and illegal. Matthew 14:1-12 reveals the scandalous details. Herodias doesn't take a liking to the reminder that she's married her brother-in-law, so as an effort to shut John up, she pressures Herod into throwing him in prison.

One night, as Herod throws a party and drinks enough to need a designated driver, he has an idea. He wants his wife's daughter, now his stepdaughter, who was once his niece, to dance for his guests. She does, and Herod likes it. In a drunken, pleasure-filled moment, Herod tells her he'll give her anything she wants, even up to half his kingdom. Unsure of what to ask for, or perhaps shocked that her mother's plan is coming together so flawlessly, she asks her mom's opinion, who, without hesitation tells her to ask for the head of John the Baptist. And for dramatic effect, she wants his head delivered to her on a platter, in front of everyone.

One moment John's minding his own business in a prison cell, locked up for doing what God told him to do, the next, he's kneeling down, laying his neck nice and still, awaiting the swoop of the blade. Just like that, he's dead. What's up with that?

John's story is extreme, and I hope that no one who reads this will ever experience what he went through. Throughout history, there have been many who've lost their life due to following Christ, and there will be more. Hopefully, for most of us, the loss will be a lot less.

Within the story of John the Baptist, there's a huge lesson to be learned, a lesson that, if you don't heed, could create a lot of frustration in your future. Holding fast to it will bring an incredible amount of peace in your life. Here it is: When things don't go according to plan, it's good to know you're just part of the plan.

God's Purpose
Trumps Our Plan

My friend, Chris, and I are standing atop South Mountain in Phoenix, Arizona. It's 2005, our adrenaline is pumping, the camera's rolling, and the satellite truck is broadcasting the signal back to our church, one thousand miles away in Oklahoma City. It's the big reveal to where our church is going to launch an additional location. Before Chris and I are to engage in a live interview with our Pastor, a video was created to build some excitement and reveal which city we are in. Because we're standing 2,300 feet above sea level in the middle of the desert on top of a mountain while staring at the camera, we can't see the roll-in video. We can tell, however, when the words, 'Phoenix, AZ' comes on the screen because that's when everyone cheers. We're all excited. As far as we know, up to this point, no one has attempted to start a church one thousand miles away by piping the sermon in via video. It's risky, innovative, and expensive. We're confident that God has called us to Phoenix and convinced it would be wildly successful.

The next three years would be difficult years. Our intent is God-honoring and faith-filled, but we make some mistakes. As a church, we assume too much and are somewhat unprepared for the challenges ahead. As a leader, my deficiencies result in a bunch of blunders and misjudgments. A few years into it, I'm repositioned, much to my relief, and ultimately the Phoenix location dissolves. It's my first real taste of failure in ministry.

Tucked away in the middle of the book of Proverbs is a verse that immediately lifts our perspective on life as a follower of Jesus. Proverbs 19:21 says, *'Many are the plans in a person's heart, but it is the Lord's purpose that prevails.'* (NIV) God is always at work on the bigger picture. Often what looks like failure is God at work, moving things further.

In Phoenix, our church learned what not to do and how to be one church in multiple (other) locations, and

 ..arned lots about leadership. One of our team members at that time now leads a growing church in the city of Phoenix. And, in the years since, by God's grace, I've had the opportunity to lead hundreds of people in Phoenix into a relationship with Jesus. In our failure lay our success. Our plan was to build a great church. God's purpose was to build his Kingdom.

'I am not...I am only...'
- John the Baptist

Before John's beheading, Jesus' ministry begins to eclipse that of John the Baptist, and some of John's followers are getting nervous. That's because Jesus is baptizing more people than John. Maybe John's supporters think he's getting lazy because their riverside attendance is dwindling. Perhaps they want to organize a leadership retreat to figure out how to course correct the mission drift and put a stop to their declining numbers. It's likely that things back then were the same as they are now; success means more.

John has a much broader perspective because he knows his role. He understands that he's just part of God's plan, and his part is to point others to Christ. When his followers get in a tizzy about Jesus attracting a larger crowd, John 3:27-28 tells us his response, *'John replied, 'No one can receive anything unless God gives it from heaven. You yourselves know how plainly I told you,*

'I am not the Messiah. I am only here to prepare the way for him."

'I am not...I am only...' That's counterintuitive in a culture where increase defines success. Continuing in John 3:29-30, John drills home his point, *'It is the bride-groom who marries the bride, and the best man is simply glad to stand with him and hear his vows. Therefore, I am filled with joy at his success. He must become greater and greater, and I must become less and less.'* John understood his role and so should we. Instead of practicing our success speech when things around us are growing, or hiding when things are in decline, maybe it's more God-honoring to say, 'I'm not the Savior. I'm only the servant.'

Only One Takes The Podium

Some guys hunt or fish, others tinker on cars or build things around the house. I cycle. If you're not familiar with cycling, I'm talking about a bicycle, not a motorcycle. Sometimes daydreaming of what might have been, it doesn't take a lot to remind me that I'll never be much more than an amateur cyclist.

I'm fascinated at the skill and athleticism of the cyclists who are the best of the best. In the Tour de France, the most prestigious race in cycling, they'll race about a hundred miles a day for twenty-one days straight with just two days off in that time frame. Over two-thousand miles at an average speed of 25-30mph in flat areas, 12-15mph while climbing some serious mountain gradients, and riding at speeds up to 40mph while sprinting toward the finish. Then there are the dangerous steep descents while traveling upwards of 60 and 70mph. Most of us have fallen off a bike, but few of us have fallen off at a rate that compares to jumping out of a car window while going down the highway.

While cycling has its heroes, the sport is a total team effort. Each team, consisting of up to nine riders, is made up of athletes with different strengths. Some are great in the condensed time trials; some are monsters climbing the mountains, while others are strong in the short, flat sprints. Even with such a large team, there's only one captain, the one whom the whole team supports and positions to win a stage of the race or the whole tour.

Rarely do the other riders expect to stand on the podium. Why? Because they know their role. They're part of the team, there to support the captain. Riding out front to break the wind and letting their team draft, carrying food for the captain so they can maintain a lighter load, or surrounding their captain so another team can't break up their pack and slow them down. The goal of the team is to put the captain on the podium as the winner.

John the Baptist knew there's only one destined for the podium, that's Jesus. On his podium, he wouldn't be hoisting a trophy, but his body high on the cross. John knew his role was to point people to Christ, to support his cause. When it comes to being a follower of Jesus, the path he leads you down may be that of asking you to do things that are more about his eternal purposes than your temporary circumstances.

Doing What's Right Is Still Right, Even When Things Go Wrong

Doing what God tells you to do is always the right thing to do. What do you do when doing what's right goes wrong? You keep doing what's right. 1 Peter 2:19-23 is encouraging to know, *'For God is pleased when, conscious of his will, you patiently endure unjust treatment. Of course, you get no credit for being patient if you are beaten for doing wrong. But if you suffer for doing good and endure it patiently, God is pleased with you. For God called you to do good, even if it means suffering, just as Christ suffered for you. He is your example, and you must follow in his steps. He never sinned, nor ever deceived anyone. He did not retaliate when he was insulted, nor threaten revenge when he suffered. He left his case in the hands of God, who always judges fairly.'*

Plans that don't go according to plan may not mean you've failed. To the contrary, there will be times when you think you've failed, but God's purpose has prevailed. When things don't go according to plan, it's good to know you're just part of the plan.

CHAPTER EIGHT

The Hater Turned Hero

YOU'VE COME THIS FAR. KEEP GOING. Beginning with the next chapter, we're going to answer our question, 'When following Jesus, what's the path he leads me down?' The answer is summed up in what we'll call The Five Essentials.

First, let's take care of some unfinished business by looking at the life of a guy who had a big choice to make, the same one we need to make if we're to go down the path where Jesus is leading.

Haters Unite!

'*And Saul approved of their killing of him.*' - Acts 8:1 (NIV). There was a man named Saul who would later change his name to Paul. A name change wasn't the only change about to happen in his life.

On a mission, he's a hunter and the followers of Jesus are his prey. An intensely religious and devout man of God, Saul's convinced that Jesus is a heretic and his goal is to prosecute his followers to the full extent of the law, even to the point of death. Acts 9:1-2 says, *'Meanwhile, Saul was uttering threats with every breath and was eager to kill the Lord's followers. So he went to the high priest. He requested letters addressed to the synagogues in Damascus, asking for their cooperation in the arrest of any followers of the Way he found there. He wanted to bring them—both men and women—back to Jerusalem in chains.'* Acts 8:3 also says, *'But Saul was going everywhere to destroy the church. He went from house to house, dragging out both men and women to throw them into prison.'*

An 'all in' kind of guy, Saul loves God, but God's doing a new thing, and he doesn't realize it. As an avid defender of the truth, Saul is about to come face to face with the one who is truth. What he doesn't recognize is that these people of 'The Way,' whom he is persecuting, have experienced what he's been looking for all of his life; a genuine encounter with the living God.

The Drive That Drove
Me To My Knees

'Scott, there's a phone call for you.' Working in a furniture store as the delivery guy, it's a cold January afternoon in Michigan when I receive the call. I have no idea who's calling. Is something wrong? Had there been an accident? On the other end of the phone is my friend, Todd. Todd had recently moved back in town after having lived in Los Angeles, California, for quite a while. 'Scott, this is Todd. I'm driving back to LA in about two weeks to pick up some stuff I left behind, would you like to go?' Living in snow covered Michigan, in the middle of winter, given the opportunity of a free trip to sunny California is an easy decision. 'Heck yeah,' is my response. Hanging up the phone, I realize I have one big problem. I have a day job. Knowing I can't get the time off to go, I do what every rational person would do, I quit and take off to Cali.

We hop into a four-wheel drive pick-up truck and head west for the 2,450-mile ride to Culver City, CA. One thing's for sure; this is going to be a blast. There's just something I'm unsure of; Todd had recently become a Jesus freak and all his talk about Jesus is starting to freak me out. I didn't know how that would play out on this trip but play out it did.

When I jump into the truck on that brisk, wintry day, I'm as far from God as one could be. Three days later, when I got out of the truck on a warm, sunny afternoon in Culver City, I'm closer to God than I'd ever been. It all started with Todd talking about his new life as a follower of Christ.

No more than a few miles into our trip and Todd is already talking about Jesus. With a lot of road ahead of us, I have no choice but to hear what he has to say. Driving south across the Michigan state line, and west onto Interstate 80, around dusk we find ourselves in the middle of an ice storm in the heart of Iowa and Nebraska. Due to the conditions, we only drive about 20mph for most of the night. The four-wheel drive is coming in handy as we motor along while everyone else has either slid into the ditch or has the smarts to get off the freeway. Driving so slow also gives Todd more time to talk, something I'm sure he enjoys.

Resistant to the Jesus stuff, by the time we make it through the night of painfully slow driving, I'm becoming curious. Experiencing a strange sense of peace, along with the hunger to hear more, Todd keeps talking. I throw out some why and what if questions and every answer's as if he's reading my mail or gazing into my soul.

Passing through Denver, CO, and into the Rocky Mountains, Todd answers all my questions, and God has gripped my heart. I'm exploding with a desire to know this Jesus. Over two days of driving across the country in a pick-up truck, I've gone from resistant to curious, to an all out epiphany.

We're just outside of Las Vegas, and I can't take it anymore; I want Christ in my life. Convinced God exists and convicted of my sin, I want a Savior, and that's Jesus. I'll never forget the moment; sitting in the cab of the truck while off in the distance I can see the lights of the Las Vegas strip. It's at that moment that I decide to surrender my life to the one who loved me and forgave me and had something more for me. I didn't know how to do that, but I knew right then and there that 'Sin City' was the beginning of my salvation. 'What happens in Vegas...', for me, would never stay in Vegas. I'd just had my very own 'Damascus Road Experience,' an encounter with Christ that required a response.

A Genuine Encounter With Christ, Genuinely Transforms Your Life

Saul's a religious thoroughbred; highly educated and incredibly dedicated, he walks the talk and is a man amongst boys. He loves God, but because God loves him, his house of cards is about to fall.

Acts 9:3-5 says, '*As he was approaching Damascus on this mission, a light from heaven suddenly shone down around him. He fell to the ground and heard a voice saying to him, 'Saul! Saul! Why are you persecuting me?' 'Who are you, lord?' Saul asked. And the voice replied, 'I am Jesus, the one you are persecuting!'*" It can happen when you least expect it, being called out by name and knocked on your can by the Son of God. Saul believes in God but has never had an experience like this. He asks, 'Who are you, lord?' Saul hears the response we all hear when choosing to look the truth in the eye, 'I am Jesus.'

There's nothing like it; your 'come to Jesus' moment. As good looking, educated, accomplished, and as impressive as you may be, everything becomes small when standing before him. A genuine encounter with Christ genuinely transforms your life. My encounter with him began with resistance (unbelieving), progressed to curiosity (wondering), and ultimately, I arrived at convinced (believing). Where are you? If you're anything like me, religion isn't an issue because you've had no religious upbringing. If you're anything like Saul, religion could be the very thing getting in the way of a fulfilling and thrilling relationship with Jesus.

Religion's a good thing when it's a God thing. James 1:27 reads, '*Religion that God our Father accepts as pure and faultless is this: to look after orphans and widows in their distress and to keep oneself from being polluted by the world.*' (NIV) Healthy religion is that of living a life devoted to God, caring for those in need, and saying no to sin. It's easy for religion to go wrong when it turns into a set of rules and behaviors designed to earn God's favor or make us look better than someone else. That leads to being self-righteous and judgmental.

When comparing his religious accomplishments to that of a relationship with his Creator, Saul, now Paul, says in Philippians 3:7-9, '*But whatever were gains to me I now consider loss for the sake of Christ. What is more, I consider everything a loss because of the surpassing worth of knowing Christ Jesus my Lord, for whose sake I have lost all things. I consider them garbage, that I may gain Christ and be found in him, not having a righteousness of my own that comes from the law, but that which is through faith in Christ-the righteousness that comes from God on the basis of faith.'* (NIV) His encounter with Christ changed his life. Later, he'd also write in 2 Corinthians 5:17, *'This means that anyone who belongs to Christ has become a new person. The old life is gone; a new life has begun!'*

An Invitation To Go Down The Path

If you've read this far, I hope you're hungry for what's next and ready to embrace The Five Essentials that every follower of Jesus is called to when following him. However, I don't want to assume you've already made the decision to follow him. If you're beyond curious and have become convinced that Jesus is who he says he is, the Son of God, I invite you to pray this simple prayer that will change your life.

'Jesus, I believe you're the Son of God. I believe you died on the cross for my sin and that you've risen from the dead. Be my Savior. I want you to be the Lord of my life, the leader of my life. I will go down the path you lead me. I'm following you with the rest of my life. Amen.'

Congratulations! Now that you've turned your life over to Christ turn the page as we discover the answer to our question, 'When following Jesus, what's the path he leads me down?'

CHAPTER NINE

ESSENTIAL #1: SURRENDER
(Letting Go)

WE'VE EXPLORED THE INCREDIBLE STORIES of a few people who've been used by God to do some extraordinary things. What God did through them is quite diverse. Some found themselves elevated to positions of leadership; some were used only for a short time to further God's purposes, while others walked through incredible pain as they played their part in what God was doing in the world.

As different as their stories are, the similarities are striking. That's where we'll now shift our focus. We could make a long list of the parallels in their lives, but long lists create clutter and are hard to apply in the real world. We're going to synthesize the list down to five similarities that were apparent in their life and are crucial in the life of everyone who's pursuing a relationship with Christ.

When following Jesus, he will lead you and I down the path of what we're calling The Five Essentials. They are surrender, obedience, service, sacrifice, and faithfulness. Though not in any specific order, there's one that's of first importance when it comes to following Jesus and fulfilling God's plan for your life; that's surrender.

The Ride Of My Life

I grabbed the handles and gave a thumbs-up. Sitting in an inner tube on a small lake in northern Michigan, I'm ready for some fun. What I'm not ready for is the ride of my life. Being pulled around a lake, bouncing off some waves, and flying over the wake behind a boat is a blast. There's just one problem with this particular ride; before giving the thumbs up, I start taunting the driver. 'No wimpy rides today. Show me what you've got.' Then, I add what no one should ever say while sitting in an inner tube on a lake tied behind a boat, 'I'll bet you can't throw me off.'

It's then that I see it in his eyes, the look of a crazed maniac given a mission. If there is ever a time I wish I could take back what I said, it's now. He guns the throttle, and my life begins flashing before my eyes. As we zoom across the lake, my teeth are rattling in my head, and every muscle in my body tenses up as the inner tube is banging off the waves. Just when I think, 'I've got this,' he banks hard to the left and whips me around to the right side of the boat. Holding on with every ounce of strength I can muster, without warning, we hit a wave that launches me into the stratosphere. Ripped out of my tube, having no time to think about what's next, I slam into the water and bounce across the surface like a pebble tossed by a child. What's most often a pleasant sensation of soft, cool, refreshing water, feels like a slab of concrete. As soon as I hit, I hear a loud 'crack,' and, starting at my neck, I feel a jolt of pain shoot through my body.

I'm never more thankful for life jackets than in this moment as I lay floating in the water, wondering if I broke my neck. For a moment I can't move, but I can feel a lot of pain. By the time the boat comes back around to get me, I'm able to move my arms and gather enough strength to do the doggy paddle swim up to the edge of the boat and pull myself in. With a throbbing headache, I have only one thought, 'I should have let go sooner.'

I learned two lessons that day; don't taunt the one who's in control of your well being, and there are moments in life when it's just better to let go.

A Surrendered Life

Let's look again at the words of Jesus from Mark 8:34-37, '*Then, calling the crowd to join his disciples, he said,*

'If any of you wants to be my follower, you must turn from your selfish ways, take up your cross, and follow me. If you try to hang on to your life, you will lose it. But if you give up your life for my sake and for the sake of the Good News, you will save it. And what do you benefit if you gain the whole world but lose your own soul? Is anything worth more than your soul?' One definition for surrender is, 'To yield to the possession or power of another.' It continues by saying, 'To give oneself up, as to the police.'

I like the typical cops and robbers TV show. Whenever the police are closing in on the bad guys, they yell, 'Freeze! Drop the weapon and put your hands in the air!' That's kind of what happens when we follow Jesus. He doesn't yell at us saying, 'Freeze! Drop your weapon...' But in a way, he does say, 'Stop! I want to take your life in a new direction. Drop everything you're holding onto, lift your hands, and surrender to me.'

A life surrendered to Christ is the call to lay it all down by holding loosely to everything that's temporary and making a priority of all things eternal. He says that there are some things we'll need to let go of; including our selfish ways. Even hanging on to things such as our dreams, our desires, and our rules for living isn't possible because his ways are so much higher than, and often contrary to ours. He then makes a promise; that if we give up our way of living for his way and his purposes, our life will be saved. We'll experience life as God meant it to be, both in this life, and the one to come.

Going All In

In elementary school, the kids in Michigan learn how to memorize the names of The Great Lakes by using the acrostic 'HOMES', which stands for Lake Huron, Ontario, Michigan, Erie, and Superior. They're the five largest lakes, by volume in the United States. As a little Michigander, we lived thirty minutes from Lake Michigan. It was a big deal when we went to the big lake. Maybe that's why I was excited the first time we took our kids to the sixth largest lake, by volume in the United States; Lake Tahoe. Our family now lives just ninety minutes from Tahoe, which is cool because people come from all over the world to visit this beautiful place, while we can make the drive up in the morning and be home before dinner.

Lake Tahoe is spectacular. Surrounded by the Sierra Nevada Mountains, sitting at 6,225 feet above sea level, Tahoe is over 1,600 feet deep. Something we quickly discovered on our first visit was how cold the water is. The annual average is around fifty degrees, and in the summer it can be in the sixties.

Our plans to plunge into the lake that day turned into a standoff of, 'I double dare ya.' Going out further than ankle deep became a test of bravery and endurance. As the kids inched their way into the water, I did my best to convince them to go all in by going all the way under the water. I told them that doing so in Lake Tahoe is something the world will envy and that they'll be able to tell the story for years to come. Yes, I exaggerated, but I wanted to see them go all in. Knowing there's no way I'd do it, maybe I was living vicariously through them.

After trying every angle of motivation, to no avail, I decided to throw in some incentive. I told our three kids that I'd give each of them $10 if they'd go all the way under the water. It's amazing how quickly the water seemed to warm up as they went under, again and again. I was out $30, but it was well worth it.

2 Corinthians 5:15 declares, *'He died for everyone so that those who receive his new life will no longer live for themselves. Instead, they will live for Christ, who died and was raised for them.'* Surrender is more than getting our feet wet; it's going all in by going all the way. Jesus gave everything to bring us into a relationship with him, and our response should be nothing less than giving everything we are back to him. When following Jesus, he leads us down the path of surrender.

Of The Five Essentials, surrender is the foundation. What is it then that we're to surrender to Christ? Are we supposed to give up everything that's fun and enjoyable? Do we commit to a life of solitude and take a vow of poverty? Does surrender mean we cancel cable TV, turn off the Wi-Fi, aim to be unpopular, out of fashion, and old-fashioned? No. Thank goodness.

The Surrender Of Sin, Self, And Our Stuff

What we do surrender to Christ is our sin, our self, and our stuff. Mark 8:34 points this out, '...*turn from your selfish ways, take up your cross, and follow me.*' We're each driven by desire, and it's important to decide which to pursue. Turning from the desires that draw us away from God, we turn to Christ and pursue our desire to know him. Doing what he says, we experience life as never before. Surrender on this level is impossible without the power of God. The beautiful thing is that what he asks us to do, he empowers us to do.

The Surrender Of Sin

Let's be honest. Sin can be fun, but it's also harmful. Natural, because it's part of our nature, sin is fueled by selfishness and is the stuff that makes a mess of life. Most of us would agree that lying, cheating, stealing, killing and abusing, etc., does damage in our life and our world. It's easy to see why we should surrender those desires to God. It's the sinful desires that don't hurt others that are often our greater enemy. Why? They're easier to hide, aren't often black and white, and their effect, though subtle, can be detrimental.

en if our behavior isn't hurting anyone else, it could be hindering our relationship with God. That's why David said in Psalm 51, *'Purify me from my sins, and I will be clean; wash me, and I will be whiter than snow. Oh, give me back my joy again...Create in me a clean heart, O God...Do not banish me from your presence, and don't take your Holy Spirit from me. Restore to me the joy of your salvation...'*

The great thing is God shows us those things that get between him and us. He does that through the teachings of Scripture and an experience called conviction. Conviction is the sense that what we're doing or about to do is either right or wrong. He makes us aware of what draws us closer to or drives us further from him. What drives us further from him is sin. The problem is, in our own strength, we are powerless to live a sinless life, yet we're responsible for our sin. Even after giving our life to Christ, this is a struggle. The Apostle Paul said in Romans 7 that his desire to sin was driving him crazy. He would later teach, *'The sinful nature wants to do evil, which is just the opposite of what the Spirit wants. And the Spirit gives us desires that are the opposite of what the sinful nature desires. These two forces are constantly fighting each other, so you are not free to carry out your good intentions.'* (Galatians 5:17) He solves the dilemma for us by saying, *'Those who belong to Christ Jesus have nailed the passions and desires of their sinful nature to his cross and crucified them there. Since we are living by the Spirit, let us follow the Spirit's leading in every part of our lives.'* (Galatians 5:24-25) Romans 8:12-13 also says, *'Therefore, dear brothers and sisters, you have no obligation to do what your sinful nature urges you to do. For if you live by its dictates, you will die. But if through the power of the Spirit you put to death the deeds of your sinful nature, you will live.'*

The Surrender Of Self

The surrender of 'self' involves our desire to control, perform, and prove our worth. These are often the deeper areas where God does some of his greatest work; where he forges our character, integrity, and sense of identity. We surrender our desire to be the god of our life; to be large and in charge, and embrace the role of a follower, a dependent child of our Creator. Victory in this space means we've stopped being god and we bow to God. When we abdicate control by no longer trying to make things happen our way, all the time, we experience the joy of watching God's plans unfold. When we cease performing for the approval of others, and especially God's approval, we rest in his grace and enjoy the peace that comes with the love of our Heavenly Father. When we no longer base our identity and self-image on the opinion of others or our opinion of ourselves, and instead, embrace who God says we are, we taste true satisfaction in life.

The Surrender Of Stuff

The surrender of our stuff complies with the truth found in Psalm 24:1, *'The earth is the Lord's, and everything in it. The world and all its people belong to him.'* Because he's the source of all we have, what we have belongs to him. Therefore, we hold our stuff loosely, ready for it to be used however he desires. We'll dig into that more during our conversation on sacrifice.

When Counting The Cost, Consider The Reward

Jesus is a straight shooter. That's part of what makes him so appealing, and polarizing. When speaking to a large crowd, he challenges them to count the cost of following him. In Luke 14:28-33, he says, *'But don't begin until you count the cost. For who would begin construction of a building without first calculating the cost to see if there is enough money to finish it? Otherwise, you might complete only the foundation before running out of money, and then everyone would laugh at you. They would say, 'There's the person who started that building and couldn't afford to finish it!' Or what king would go to war against another king without first sitting down with his counselors to discuss whether his army of 10,000 could defeat the 20,000 soldiers marching against him? And if he can't, he will send a delegation to discuss terms of*

peace while the enemy is still far away. So you cannot be-
come my disciple without giving up everything you own.'

A life surrendered to Christ is the call to lay it all down; to let go of anything that gets in the way of knowing God more. It's holding loosely to everything that's temporary and making a priority of all things eternal. Every time God wants you and me to surrender something, he's persuading us to pursue more of him. Whatever the cost, it's worth it.

Being surrendered to Christ leads us to the next place where Jesus leads us, a life of obedience.

CHAPTER TEN

ESSENTIAL #2: OBEDIENCE
(The Better Way)

She Asked The Question And I Didn't Know What To Say

AFTER A BRUTAL BEATING, in a humiliating fashion, he's nailed to a cross and propped up for all to see. The gawkers, critics, and confused followers look on as he gasps for each breath. Six hours pass, and finally, with one last exhale it's over. A few days later, he has a lot to say.

Risen and facing a band of mesmerized, rag-tag disciples, Jesus says something that would forever change how billions of people live their lives, *'All authority in heaven and on earth has been given to me. Therefore go and make disciples of all nations, baptizing them in the*

name of the Father and of the Son and of the Holy Spirit,
and teaching them to obey everything I have commanded
you. And surely I am with you always, to the very end of
the age.' (Matthew 28:18-20 NIV)

Referred to as The Great Commission, those words
are what motivated a few of my friends and me to head
downtown to a nightclub called the Reptile House. The
epitome of all things grunge, underground, rebellious,
and anti-establishment, the Reptile House was the last
place where someone would expect to have a conversation about Jesus.

On this particular Saturday night, when we arrive,
there are people lined up all the way down the sidewalk, waiting to get in. Thinking we have a captive audience, we mingle with everyone in line, trying to
strike up a discussion about life, faith, and other popu-
lar nightclub topics like eternity. It doesn't take long to
discover that most of them are more interested in paying their cover charge and getting inside for a night of
partying than they are in talking about God.

Discouraged and ready to give up, I'm near the back
of the line when a girl seems interested in what I have
to say. Probably around twenty years old, inquisitive,
and kind, she asks me a question that catches me off
guard. In a very matter-of-fact way, she asks, 'If I believe in Jesus, do I have to obey him?'

I don't know what to say. Conflicted and confused, I
assume she wants to debate about religion and why it
turns her off. The last thing I want to talk about is rules
and regulations and other things that religious people

argue over. I want her to get a glimpse of how much God loves her, how His grace and forgiveness is available to her, and how she can experience the new life that comes through a relationship with Jesus. I don't want to scare her off by saying something that might shut down the conversation.

Processing how to respond, I almost say, 'Following Jesus isn't about being obedient,' but as quick as the thought comes to mind, I know I can't because a couple of Bible verses come to mind that challenge me to stay true to what I know. Misleading her would not be beneficial. Grabbing my little pocket Bible, I open it up to John 14:15, and show her the words of Jesus where he says, *'If you love me, obey my commandments.'* Taking it a bit further and jumping down a few verses to John 14:23-24, I read, *'Jesus replied, 'All who love me will do what I say....Anyone who doesn't love me will not obey me.'*

I'll never forget her response. After showing her those Scriptures, she says, 'OK. No thanks.' The conversation is over.

When following Christ, he will lead you down the path of obedience. In fact, the path of following Jesus is paved with obedience. In a world of nonconformity and independence, 'obey' has become a four-letter word. A rebel at heart, and someone who believes rules are meant to be broken; I see why obedience can be a hard pill to swallow. It's easy to view a commanding God as a demanding God; telling us to embrace a particular belief system and a set of behaviors while forcing his will on us by requiring obedience. That's not a relationship built on grace; that's submission based on fear. Understanding the purpose behind God's commands changes our thoughts about obedience because whenever God tells us to do something, he has our best interest in mind.

The Better Way

Every command from God is designed to get you where he wants you to be. His call to obey is an invitation to go the better way. It's been a few years since I've read through the whole Bible, from start to finish, so, this year I decided to do just that. A couple of months into it, something jumped out at me. I was somewhere deep in the book of Exodus when the thought occurred to me, 'Wow, God's people have always been a mess.' In a way, that realization was encouraging because I then thought, 'Good, I'm not alone.'

Reading through the Old Testament, we see how patiently, and mercifully God continues to lead his people, to provide for them, and deliver them while they go on disobeying his commands and disregarding all he's done for them. In the book of Exodus, God's power is on display as he performs miracle after miracle while delivering his people from four hundred years of slavery in Egypt. Once they cross the Red Sea, in what should have been an eleven-day journey to their promised land, they spend the next forty years wandering in the desert. Forty years! Why? Disobedience. God tells them what to do to get them where he wants them to go, but because they wouldn't comply with his commands, he lets them wander through the desert, wading in their disobedience.

It's shocking how much obedience and disobedience to God's commands have determined the course of history. Going all the way back to the beginning, in Genesis 2:16-17, God tells Adam and Eve, '*You may freely eat the fruit of every tree in the garden-except the tree of the knowledge of good and evil. If you eat its fruit, you are sure to die.*' Having everything they'd ever need, including God's presence on a daily basis, they're told to obey only one command; not to eat the fruit from just one tree. If they do, they die. In chapter three Satan comes along and tempts Eve to eat from the tree while Adam is right there with her. They both eat the fruit and their act of disobedience opens the floodgate for sin to enter the world. One moment of disobedience sets in motion the fall of humanity.

What's even more amazing is how God fixes the dilemma brought on by disobedience. Romans 5:19 says, '*For just as through the disobedience of the one man the many were made sinners, so also through the obedience of the one man the many will be made righteous.*' God's plan of redemption is an act of obedience. As Jesus obeys his Father's plan, it brings him right where he's supposed to be, on the cross. Through one deed of disobedience sin surges through humankind, and through one epic moment of obedience the door to grace is opened for us all.

It's important to understand that obedience isn't performance. Scripture is very clear that our relationship with God depends on grace, through faith, it's his gift to us - Ephesians 2:8. God's love, the forgiveness he extends to us, and the acceptance we have as his children is based entirely on Christ's work on the cross.

What part then does obedience play? Remember when Jesus said, *'If you love me, obey my commandments.'* It's one of the ways we express love back to God. Obedience also brings spiritual and emotional health into our life because when we obey him, we're living in alignment with his design. Also, don't forget that every command from God is intended to get us where he wants us to be. How do we follow Jesus? One step of obedience at a time. Obedience never has and never will go out of style. Obedience always goes well with whatever life brings our way.

Obedience Brings You Through The Storms

Jesus concludes his famous 'Sermon on the Mount', by telling a short parable beginning in Matthew 7:24, *'Anyone who listens to my teaching and follows it is wise, like a person who builds a house on solid rock. Though the rain comes in torrents and the floodwaters rise and the winds beat against that house, it won't collapse because it is built on bedrock. But anyone who hears my teaching and doesn't obey it is foolish, like a person who builds a house on sand. When the rains and floods come and the winds beat against that house, it will collapse with a mighty crash.'* (Matthew 7:24-27)

I have to admit there are times when reading the Bible that I wish I could change what it says. This Scripture is one. I'd rather Matthew 7:24-25 say, *'Anyone who listens to my teaching and follows it is wise, like a person who builds a house on solid rock. If you do what I say, the storms of life will blow south around your house (life) and never come close to touching you or those you love.'* Wouldn't that be better? Ironically, this is what many of us believe, and it's caused a lot of confusion and frustration.

Jesus doesn't say that obeying his teaching will result in a storm-free life, but he does say it will create a stormproof life. When the economy crashes, the company downsizes, your marriage struggles, your kids go crazy, or worse, tragedy hits, those who obey his teaching will still be standing once the storms pass. Obedience doesn't create immunity to trials, but it does provide a compass to navigate them.

The storms of life can do enormous damage and leave behind lots of debris; pain, disappointment, loss, confusion, and debt. Surrounded by that kind of rubble, how does obedience to the teachings of Jesus help us stand? We saw how God brought Joseph, Job, John the Baptist, and Paul through great trials. It's not the intensity of the storm that determines if we stand or fall; it's

our obedience to God's Word that creates the foundation to stand on and gives us the strength to get
through. When the storms come, stay the course of
surrender and obedience. Through the storms your
faith can remain steady, your intimacy with Christ can
increase, and you'll see life more clearly because you
will crave eternity more intensely.

In this parable, two guys have two things in common. They each hear the teachings of Jesus, and experience storms. What they don't have in common is
their response; one obeys and the other doesn't. The
result? One withstands the storms of life, and the other
crashes.

Building A Solid Foundation

Jesus gives us two clear steps in this parable that help to
build a stormproof life when he says, '*Anyone who listens to my teaching and follows it is wise...*' First, we are
to listen to his teaching. Second, we are to do what he
says. We can't do what he says if we don't know what
he says. And what's the use of knowing what he says if
we're not interested in doing what he says?

A follower of Christ loves God's Word. It's a part of
our everyday life; reading it casually, studying it intensely, hanging on it's every word. Psalm 119:47-
48 says, '*How I delight in your commands! How I love
them! I honor and love your commands. I meditate on
your decrees.*'

A follower of Christ lives God's Word. According to Jesus, we can't go any deeper than obedience. When reading the Bible, we should ask ourselves, 'Is there a command to obey?' James 1:22-25 emphasizes this by saying, *'But don't just listen to God's word. You must do what it says. Otherwise, you are only fooling yourselves. For if you listen to the word and don't obey, it is like glancing at your face in a mirror. You see yourself, walk away, and forget what you look like. But if you look carefully into the perfect law that sets you free, and if you do what it says and don't forget what you heard, then God will bless you for doing it.'* Listening to God's word without the intent to live God's word is how we fool ourselves. Hearing the truth can calm and encourage our troubled heart, but it's obedience that will change our life.

Bust Through The Obstacles Of Obedience

The greatest obstacle to obedience is fear. It not only gets in the way, but it also creates a separate path. When facing the decision to obey or go another way, don't trust the strongest pull, trust God. The path of obedience can be scary and full of uncertainty, but God is trustworthy. Though sometimes hard, obedience moves you forward in God's plan for your life. Don't allow the fear of failure, loss, or rejection to sidetrack you into the rut of disobedience. It may seem the easier way to go, but disobedience is always a step backward.

1 Samuel 15:22 says, '*What is more pleasing to the Lord: your burnt offerings and sacrifices or your obedience to his voice? Listen! Obedience is better than sacrifice...*' When afraid, obey anyway.

Another obstacle to obedience is needing to know why. When our kids were young, I'd tell them to do something without giving much explanation. At three years old, 'Don't run into the street,' and, 'Eat your vegetables,' was enough to keep them alive and growing. If they asked, 'Why?', I'd often respond, 'Because I said so.' As they grew, Shelly and I would take the time to explain 'why' because we were trying to expand their perspective and teach them how to make good decisions.

There will be times when God tells you to do something, and you'll want to know why. He may speak to you through the still small voice of the Holy Spirit, or through a direct command in Scripture, and you'll ask, 'Why?' Don't be surprised if he responds, 'Because I said so.' He's the father; you're the child. He knows more than you and will always have the greater perspective because he sees the end from the beginning. Of course, there will be times when God explains why because he's teaching you something through your obedience. However, if he gives no explanation, just do it.

As a follower of Christ, obedience is non-negotiable. To experience God's best, listen to what he has to say and do what he says. Every command from God is designed to get you where he wants you to be and his call to obey is an invitation to go the better way.

I sometimes wonder what happened to that girl standing outside the Reptile House that night. Did she ever come to know of God's love and grace? Did she ever realize that his commands are there because he cares? I wish we could talk again and I wish she'd ask that same question, 'If I believe in Jesus, do I have to obey him?' With excitement, I'd say, 'Not only do you have to, you get to.'

CHAPTER ELEVEN

ESSENTIAL #3: SERVICE
(A Servant Of All)

Our Tussle With Tornado Alley

THE PEOPLE IN OKLAHOMA ARE GOOD PEOPLE. You're already acquainted with Kevin, who said to me, 'God's going to break you,' but let me introduce you to another Kevin, the one who said something that eased one of my greatest fears. I asked him the question that everyone asks an Oklahoman when they're in the Sooner State, 'Do tornadoes pass through here?'

Our family had just moved into the mid-sized town of Edmond, Oklahoma. It's a great place, everything you'd expect from a community of about one-hundred-thousand people in middle America; good schools, nice restaurants, lots of churches, and, I was hoping, no tornadoes. I don't know if Kevin could discern the concern in my voice, but his reply calmed my anxious thoughts. 'Not really,' he said, 'The last time I remember a tornado coming through this area was about thirteen years ago.' Two weeks later, the thirteen-year tornado dry spell would be over.

What begins as an average afternoon in March 2008 becomes a day that is forever engraved in the memory of the Rodgers family. Tornadoes do pass through Edmond, and the first one in thirteen years is heading straight for our house.

Earlier in the day, the meteorologists are saying the weather is conducive for tornadoes. The weather folks in Oklahoma know their stuff, and when they say storms are probable, you'd better take it to heart. In a very informative fashion, they pick apart weather patterns as if they're five-point sermons on the nature and deity of Christ. It's mesmerizing. Their rhetorical eloquence and theatrical presence are almost intoxicating as they discuss high and low-pressure systems, cold fronts, warm fronts, dry lines, wall clouds, hook echoes, and the periodic tales of lore from their storied tornadic past.

Everyone in the office that day is keeping an eye on the weather. By the end of the workday, I can see the darkness approaching from the southwestern horizon. In that part of the country, most tornadoes travel from the southwest toward the northeast. After a short drive home, I walk into the house where Shelly has the TV tuned into the weather report. Tornadoes are touching down about one hundred miles away, and the same storm front is heading in our direction. It seems just a matter of time, but much to our surprise, a couple of hours later, the storms begin to dissipate, and it looks like we're in the clear. At 11:00 pm we go to bed, looking forward to a peaceful night's rest.

Right around midnight, I wake up to the noise of tornado sirens and rain beating against the house. I jump up and turn the TV on to hear that a tornado has just touched down southwest of Oklahoma City. Not long after, the meteorologist says that another funnel is nearing the corner of 2nd Street and Pennsylvania Avenue in Edmond. He then speaks the words I'd feared, the words that Kevin said hadn't been voiced in thirteen years, 'Folks, if you're in the area of 2nd and Penn in Edmond, take cover immediately.' The funnel is exactly one mile southwest of our house. Which way do tornadoes travel? That's right; we are right in the line of fire.

Running through the house, Shelly and I split up to get our three kids out of bed and into the master bedroom closet. Ashley and Morgan walk themselves into the closet while I have to carry Dylan because he won't wake up. Huddling together, the kids ask, 'Dad, are we going to be ok?' That's when we begin to pray.

With hail pounding on the house and wind whistling through the patio door, as quickly as it started, it stops. Not a sound. Shelly asks, 'Is that it?' 'I think so,' I say. 'Let me check. You guys stay here.' Walking out of the closet, making my way into the kitchen, I look past the dining table through a big window into the backyard. The power is out, and it's pitch-black inside and outside. Apart from using a flashlight, I can't see a thing. The air is eerily still, and everything's quiet.

Without warning, the house begins to shake. Unsure of what's happening, I instinctively run back through the house and into the bedroom closet, like a little girl running for her life. The walls start rattling; we're bunched together and scared to death. It sounds like a freight train is going through our backyard.

A few moments later, it's silent again. Alive, but white as a sheet, one of the kids asks, 'Was that it? Is it over?' After waiting a minute or two, I once again tell them to stay put while I go to the kitchen to take a look outside. This time, everything is different. I can see our neighbors moving around, inspecting the damage. It takes me a moment to realize that's a sight I shouldn't be able to see. The big wooden fence surrounding our yard is gone, never to be found. Debris is laying around, and some rooftops are damaged. The good news is no one's hurt. It was a small tornado, probably on the scale of an F1 or F2. Down the road from us, there's a neighborhood that took a direct hit with a lot of damage and a home that is destroyed.

The next day the people from our church knew what to do. 1 John 3:17-18 says, *'If anyone has material possessions and sees a brother or sister in need but has no pity on them, how can the love of God be in that person? Dear children, let us not love with words or speech but with actions and in truth.'* (NIV)

It's time to get to work. It's time to serve.

Descending Into Greatness

When following Christ, he will lead you down the path of serving others.

James and John, two of Jesus' disciples, were much like you and me; when perceiving an opportunity for position and power might come their way, it was hard to resist. Gaining momentum and increasing in numbers, many of the followers of Jesus believed it was just a matter of time before he'd rise to political rule. Assuming that he'd place those closest to him into positions of influence, James and John, with a little help from their mama, asked Jesus if they could sit in the highest places of honor, on his right and his left, when he sat on the throne.

Their request didn't sit well with the rest of Jesus' followers. Before dealing James and John some humble pie, he first had to settle everyone down because the political posturing was making them angry. In Matthew 20:25-28 Jesus addresses their frustration by saying, *'You know that the rulers in this world lord it over their people, and officials flaunt their authority over those under them. But among you it will be different. Whoever wants to be a leader among you must be your servant, and whoever wants to be first among you must become your slave.*

For even the Son of Man came not to be served but to serve others and to give his life as a ransom for many.'

According to Jesus, the greatest position in His Kingdom is that of serving others. If you want to be the big kahuna, you'll have to be the chief servant. 1 Peter 4:10 emphasizes that God has gifted each of us with the goal of serving, *'God has given each of you a gift from his great variety of spiritual gifts. Use them well to serve one another.'* Not only are we gifted to serve, but our attitude toward serving is also to reflect the words of Jesus in Matthew 7:12, *'Do to others whatever you would like them to do to you. This is the essence of all that is taught in the law and the prophets.'*

The Day I Did Nothing

Christians aren't the only people who serve others. I have some friends who don't follow Christ that are doing great things by serving others. Our communities are full of good people who care and who are working hard to make someone's life better. You don't have to be a Christian to care about the needs of others, but can you be a Christian and not care?

Several years ago I was sitting in my home office at about 8:00 am, on a Friday morning. Focused on my computer screen, I didn't realize what was happening across the street. Cars were lining up all the way down the road, and people were walking into our neighbor's house. Keeping to themselves, we'd never made much of a connection with these particular neighbors. They were a married couple with two kids; one, a younger boy, and the other, a girl in high school. It struck me as odd that so many people would be visiting them this early in the morning. It wasn't the day for the annual neighborhood garage sale, just a bunch of people quietly walking down the street and going into their home.

Not until later in the afternoon did I hear what happened. The day before, their daughter was in a car accident while coming home from school. She'd passed away. One of the worst things that could happen happened.

In response, I did one of the worst things I've ever done; I did nothing. So afraid of not knowing what to say or how to say it, I instead chose to remain silent and turn the other way. It was one of the biggest failures of my Christian life. To this day, I'm ashamed of what I didn't do. Sure, it would have been a long walk across the street and an awkward conversation to have, but that's no excuse to do nothing. Maybe that's why I'm convinced it's impossible to get close to the heart of God while remaining apathetic toward the needs of those around us.

Embrace The Inconvenience
Of Serving Others

In Luke 10:25, a religious guy tries to test Jesus by asking an important question, *'Teacher, what must I do to inherit eternal life?'* Jesus responds by asking him what he thinks the answer is. Mr. Religious replies, *'You must love the Lord your God with all your heart, all your soul, all your strength, and all your mind.' And, 'Love your neighbor as yourself.''* (Luke 10:27) *'Right! Do this and you will live!',* Jesus tells him.

In an attempt to justify his actions, Mr. Religious then asks a question that ruins it for the rest of us because Jesus launches into a teaching moment that would forever eliminate every excuse not to serve others. He tells the story of a Jewish guy who's traveling down a dangerous stretch of road between Jerusalem and Jericho. While in route, he's jumped by a bunch of thugs. Beat up, stripped naked, lying in a ditch, and left for dead, two religious guys then come along, both Jewish. The first one sees him, and choosing to look the other way, he crosses to the other side of the road and continues toward his destination. The second guy does the same. Along comes a third man, a Samaritan. It's important to note that Jews and Samaritan's didn't get along and didn't go out of their way for one another. Jesus says that he; the most unlikely of the three, has compassion and chooses to help. Bandaging him up, he takes the wounded to receive medical care and pays the bill.

When crossing paths with someone who's fallen on bad times, hurt, or in need, as followers of Jesus, we're called to do something. Serving others may be inconvenient because it disrupts our schedule. Sometimes that something will spoil our plans for a day, or two, or longer. Occasionally, doing what's necessary to help will also cost us something. Luke 10:35 says of the Samaritan, *'The next day he handed the innkeeper two silver coins, telling him, 'Take care of this man. If his bill runs higher than this, I'll pay you the next time I'm here.'* 'I'll pray for you,' is a good start, but 'I'll pay for you,' may also be required.

Jesus brings it home by challenging Mr. Religious, *'Now which of these three would you say was a neighbor to the man who was attacked by bandits?' Jesus asked. The man replied, 'The one who showed him mercy.' Then Jesus said, 'Yes, now go and do the same.'* (Luke 10:36-37)

Would you like to see God at work in your life? Become the work of God in someone else's life. James 2:14-17 says, *'What good is it, dear brothers and sisters, if you say you have faith but don't show it by your actions? Can that kind of faith save anyone? Suppose you see a brother or sister who has no food or clothing, and you say, "Good-bye and have a good day; stay warm and eat well"— but then you don't give that person any food or clothing. What good does that do? So you see, faith by itself isn't enough. Unless it produces good deeds, it is dead and useless.'* Being a follower of Christ is more than what you believe, it's adopting a lifestyle, being devoted to the way of life as taught by Jesus. Knowing what he teaches is important. Living what he teaches is imperative.

Where To Start?

There's an old saying, 'Find a need and fill it. Find a hurt and heal it.' Much like Jesus' story about the Samaritan, the opportunity to serve others often finds you. Other times, you'll need to look for ways to serve. Regardless, those who are following Jesus will be found serving others.

With so much need in the world, it's easy to become overwhelmed with it all. It helps to get your eyes off the masses and focus on the one. I once heard someone say, 'You can't do something for everyone, but you can do something for someone.' God may or may not use you to change the world, but he'll use you to change someone's life. One way to serve is through the local church. You don't even need to pray about it. Ephesians 4:16 makes it clear by saying, '*He makes the whole body fit together perfectly. As each part does its own special work, it helps the other parts grow, so that the whole body is healthy and growing and full of love.*' Serving one another as the church is also one way that God has chosen to reach the world. In John 13:35, Jesus says, '*Your love for one another will prove to the world that you are my disciples.*' Get involved in what God is doing through your church.

There are plenty of opportunities to serve outside of the church too. Schools, community organizations, sports teams, and service clubs are just a few. Then, there's your next door neighbor, the family across the street, and the people you sit next to at the little league baseball game. As you serve, keep in mind the purpose behind all you do, which is to participate in fulfilling God's purposes for the world. Love him with all your heart, love people with all your might, and introduce others to Christ as you serve. *'In the same way, let your light shine before others, that they may see your good deeds and glorify your Father in Heaven.'* (Matthew 5:16 NIV)

CHAPTER TWELVE

ESSENTIAL #4: SACRIFICE
(Going Without)

The Day We Bet The Farm

WITH OUR HEADS BOWED, EYES CLOSED, and hearts wide open to doing whatever God might tell us to do, we had no idea that, only moments later, Shelly and I would be making the most irrational decision we'd ever made.

Just having walked away from her career as an accountant, Shelly is focusing on the full-time job of being a first-time mom. Overnight, our income is cut in half. To add anxiety to uncertainty, I had just walked away from full-time work to take a part-time job to start an internship at our church.

A ministry internship is a boot camp for pastor wannabe's, where you're used and abused while doing anything and everything needed usually at a fast-paced, understaffed church. On pay day, as an intern, you thank the Lord that he's on your side because you make about the same amount of money as you would standing on a street corner with a guitar, singing for those passing by.

We'd done the math and knew there'd be more month left over than money, and here we are, sitting in church praying about giving away some cold hard cash to a worthy cause. Already investing ten percent of our income into the work of the local church, we could say enough is enough, but we're wondering if we can help even more.

After praying, we open our eyes, lift our heads, and look at each other, waiting to see who'd make the first move. I have a particular amount in mind that I think we should give but am too scared to say what it is. Staring at one another, I ask, 'What do you believe we should give?' Hoping she'll say something entirely different, and a lot less than what I'm thinking, Shelly isn't going to let me off the hook that easy. She replies, 'What do you say we should give?'

Isn't it funny how touchy the topic of money is when it comes to our faith? Maybe that's because of how it's been abused. We've all heard stories of an imposter who's in it for the money, pedaling religious goods and services as a means of raking in the dough. Like dope dealers, they're hope dealers, manipulating emotions and preying on people's desire to know God and do his will. As sad as that is, I think there's also another reason we're sensitive about money and faith. It's the great rivalry of the heart. Jesus says in Matthew 6:24, '*No one can serve two masters. For you will hate one and love the other; you will be devoted to one and despise the other. You cannot serve both God and money.*' Money, and what we do with it, always brings us back to the matter of surrender.

It's at this moment that Shelly and I have the decision to make; are we going to remain surrendered to God and what we believe he's telling us to do? With nowhere to run and no place to hide, I have to decide. Will I say to Shelly what I think God is saying to me, or, will I allow my fear to voice itself by going low and trusting in our supply instead of our supplier? In one forceful step of faith, I go for it and say, 'Three Thousand Dollars.' Not knowing if she's going to slap me or start crying, to my shock, Shelly says, 'That's exactly what I was thinking.'

After walking away from half our income, we're now giving away half our life's savings. One-half, minus another half is going to be one colossal mistake or one big step forward toward where God is leading us. We aren't sure, but we write the check, wave bye-bye to our sense of security, and go all in on what we want our lives to represent. Is God going to take care of us or not? We'd never know if we held on to all we had.

'To Whom It May Concern' - God

When following Christ, he will lead you down the path of sacrifice.

Ephesians 5:1-2 reads, '*Imitate God, therefore, in everything you do. Live a life filled with love, following the example of Christ. He loved us and offered himself as a sacrifice for us, a pleasing aroma to God.*' We imitate God by following Christ's example of loving others at a level that requires sacrifice. Beyond just money, it's the giving of our time, abilities, life experience, know-how, and our stuff.

The Apostle Paul, who wrote the book of Ephesians, practiced what he preached when quoting Jesus in one of the most well-known verses in the Bible, '*And I have been a constant example of how you can help those in need by working hard. You should remember the words of the Lord Jesus: 'It is more blessed to give than receive.*'" (Acts 20:35)

Understanding the value of every human being and grasping the gravity of eternity is the driving force behind sacrifice. It's choosing to go without so that others can experience the love, power, and provision of God in their life. Giving away what you need to meet the needs of someone else while embracing temporary pain to help heal somebody's hurt. Missing a meal to feed one who's hungry, leaving something undone in your life to care for the weak, or being vulnerable to backlash because of sharing your faith are all examples of sacrifice. Serving is normal, sacrifice is exceptional, both are a way of life for a follower of Christ.

Jesus had something to say about this in Matthew 25:31-46. In vivid and sobering fashion, he says there will come a time when everyone stands in his presence, and God will separate us like a shepherd separates the sheep from the goats. The sheep will go to his right, which is where you want to go, and the goats to the left, which is where you don't want to go. A determining factor of which side people will go comes from what they did for the hungry, the thirsty, the stranger, the naked, the sick, and those in prison. In Matthew 25:34-35, telling those who are the 'sheep', he says, *'Come, you who are blessed by my Father, inherit the Kingdom pre-pared for you from the creation of the world. For I was hungry, and you fed me. I was thirsty, and you gave me a drink. I was a stranger, and you invited me into your home. I was naked, and you gave me clothing. I was sick, and you cared for me. I was in prison, and you visited me.'* Not un-derstanding what he meant because they'd never fed him or visited him in prison, etc., they ask, when did we do any of that? Jesus replies, *'I tell you the truth, when you did it to one of the least of these my brothers and sisters, you were doing it to me!'* (Matthew 25:40) What we do for those in need is part of the conversation when we step into eternity.

A Saint, A Stork, And A Reminder That God Would Provide

Her voice is cracking, and I can tell she's crying when I answer the phone. Shelly says, 'The doctor said I need to go to the emergency room, immediately. Can you come home and take me to the hospital?' Diagnosed with meningitis, the pain in her head is severe, and she's almost passing out. The doctor says he can't tell if it's viral or bacterial meningitis, both are bad but bacterial is worse. That's why he demands we get to the hospital fast, to determine which it is.

I stop everything, speed home, and rush her to the hospital. Taking the shortest route possible while ignoring the speed limit, we don't know what will happen when we get there. What we do know is the timing couldn't be worse. As you remember, Shelly has just quit her job, I've transitioned from full-time work with insurance benefits to my poverty level internship, and we're scared to death about how much this is going to cost.

After getting a spinal tap, the doctor tells us that it's viral, not bacterial. That's the good news. The bad news; the bill is on the way.

The very next day someone knocks on our door. It's a woman that Shelly has met once or twice at a Bible study, and there's no reason why this 'stranger' should be at our door. Standing there, very nervous, she says, 'I've never done this before, and I'm not sure if I'm doing this right, but I think God spoke to me and told me to stop by your house to give you this.' She hands Shelly a bag of groceries and a fifty-dollar bill. We are beside ourselves with gratitude. Fifty dollars won't touch the medical bill, but it shoots our faith to the moon. Not a full day has gone by before God reminds us that he's our provider. That lady, a timid saint, became to us a stork from heaven. A few days later, my previous employer, the one I left to take the internship, decides to continue our medical coverage and pay for it long enough to cover the cost of the hospital visit. Then, without asking for help, a group of friends give us money that would eventually pay for the additional expenses of our insurance deductible and some lost wages. Within in a matter of a few weeks, everything is paid in full.

This story isn't an infomercial promising an extravagant life for three easy payments of $19.99. This example is about God being your provider when you sacrificially provide for others. 2 Corinthians 9:7-8 says, 'You must each decide in your heart how much to give. And don't give reluctantly or in response to pressure. 'For God loves a person who gives cheerfully.' And God will generously provide all you need. Then you will always have everything you need and plenty left over to share with others." When you pour out your life for the cause of Christ by offering up what you have to meet the needs of others, you can stand in the confidence of Psalm 34:10 that says, 'Even strong young lions sometimes go *hungry, but those who trust in the Lord will lack no good thing.'*

A Level Of Giving That Impacts Your Standard Of Living

Serving and sacrifice go hand in hand. However, not all serving requires sacrifice. Blocking out a half-day here and there, volunteering an hour or two, once a week, or rearranging a vacation schedule isn't sacrifice. The stakes are higher when sacrifice is required. Sacrifice is giving what you need to someone God wants to reach. It's a level of giving that affects your standard of living.

Maybe this year's year-end-bonus isn't for you. Perhaps God wants it to go through you to someone who needs it even more. If so, he'll let you know. That's sacrifice. Exhausted after a hard day's work, you spend your evenings with a friend, for a season, because their life's falling apart and they need you. With dirty dishes on the counter and laundry piling up, you choose the hurting over the to-do list; that's sacrifice. For some, you could be making more money doing something other than what God is calling you to do with your life's work; that's sacrifice. Taking a stand for your convictions and losing the sale because of it; that's sacrifice. Working less to put your relationship with your family first; that's sacrifice. Giving your sandwich to someone who forgot his or her lunch, while your stomach is yelling at you; that's sacrifice. You don't have to hang on a cross to live a sacrificial life, but you will have to give up something you need for someone God wants to reach.

Share Your Fries

'Can I have some fries?' We'd done this before; swing through the drive-thru for a quick snack to hold the kids over until dinner. Thinking they're going to die of starvation because they haven't eaten for three hours, they talk me into buying them some French fries on the way home. As soon as I pass back the three orders of fries, the complaints of hunger and parental abuse go silent as they go into a deep-fried food coma. It's amazing how delicious those fries are when one thinks they're having visions of the afterlife and expecting to step over the edge of eternity at any moment because they missed breakfast or snack time.

As the parent, or should I say chauffeur, the smell of fresh, hot fries in the car is like that of an intoxicating perfume. As the scent moves its way back toward the front, it crawls up the back of your seat, over your shoulders, whispering, 'I know you want me.' That's when your stomach screams and you say to your children, 'Can I have some fries?'

Thinking they must know that I'm the one who bought the fries, I'm hoping to hear, 'Of course, dad. You paid for these fries, and without you, we wouldn't be eating them right now. How many would you like, oh gracious and loving father?' Not so. Without looking up, they each say, 'Not mine. I don't have enough. You can have some of Ashley's,' or whichever sibling they think of first. At this moment, all of my parenting failures flash before my eyes.

All I want are a few fries, the fries I paid for with my hard earned money. Now, I'm not thinking only about how I can grab all the fries out of their greedy little hands without crashing the car; I'm wondering how to ship them off to boarding school. The selfish little beasts with darkened hearts won't even share a few fries, the fries I paid for in the first place. Eventually, I command them to give me some fries or they'll be walking home, but I no longer enjoy them because I had to pry them out of their miserly hands.

Sacrificing something of ours for the sake of helping others isn't so hard when we realize we're just sharing what God has given us. What we have comes from him. 1 Timothy 6:17-19 tells us, '*Command those who are rich in this present world not to be arrogant nor to put their hope in wealth, which is so uncertain, but to put their hope in God, who richly provides us with everything for our enjoyment. Command them to do good, to be rich in good deeds, and to be generous and willing to share. In this way they will lay up treasure for themselves as a firm foundation for the coming age, so that they may take hold of the life that is truly life.*' The next time you're faced with the opportunity to sacrifice, just remember, your Father is asking you to share your fries.

ESSENTIAL #5: FAITHFULNESS
(Sticking With It)

The Honeymoon From Hades

ON AUGUST 19, 1995, I LOOKED SHELLY in the eyes and said, 'I promise to be your loving and faithful husband. I will be faithful to you in good times and bad, sickness and health. I will love you and honor you, protect and provide for you, all the days of my life.' Ten hours later, I would test her commitment to doing the same for me.

I earlier shared what Shelly and I did when returning from our honeymoon by moving into the rough area of town. What I didn't tell was what happened on our honeymoon. It's not what you're thinking. There's no need to cover the eyes and ears of the children. In fact, if you have kids, you may want to read this to them, so they know what stupid looks like.

Once engaged, Shelly and I decide to divide up the duties; she's responsible for planning the wedding, and I'm in charge of putting together the honeymoon. The wedding goes off without a hitch while the honeymoon, well; let's just say things don't go so smoothly. Our plan is to spend a wonderful week relaxing in Cape Cod, Massachusetts. Living in Michigan, we decide to drive the short one-thousand-mile trek around the south side of Lake Erie and across the beautiful rolling hills of Pennsylvania. Going around New York City, we'll turn north, up the Eastern Seaboard and into historic Cape Cod, with 'Just Married' written on the back window and tin cans dangling from the bumper.

The day we both say, 'I do,' turns into the day we both think, 'I don't know if we're gonna make it.' That's because I'm probably the first guy in the history of modern day weddings that decides to 'wing it' for the honeymoon. That's right, other than an eventual arrival into Cape Cod; my game plan is to have no other plans; no hotel reservations, no scheduled stops along the way, no forethought for exotic beach exploits, nothing. The idea is to get in the car and head east. For me, that's the epitome of romance and adventure. To Shelly, such a plan is reckless and irresponsible. As you might imagine, things don't go so well.

The first night of our honeymoon is quite memorable. It begins with the wedding planner forgetting to have the pastor sign the marriage certificate. Realizing we aren't legally married until it's signed, about four hours after the wedding, we call him on the phone asking if he'd come back to sign it. Exhausted from the stress of the wedding, a photo shoot, and the reception, once the pastor made it back and made things legal, we hit the road. It's around dusk when we make it into Ohio. Deciding to stop for the night, we pull off the freeway and into a hotel parking lot only to discover there's no room at the inn. Due to a big stock car race and a huge tractor pull event in the region, the hotels are all booked, from Detroit to New York. Struggling to continue and knowing that falling asleep at the wheel on our first night of marriage wouldn't be the best beginning to a life together, we pull into a rest stop in Cleveland.

The view is unforgettable. The smokestacks, the shimmer of industrial lighting, and the sights and sounds of steel mills in Cleveland become the canvas on which we begin making life-long memories.

We get out of the car to stretch our legs and realize enjoying what's left of the night is no longer possible, that surviving until morning is our new goal. On this night, I, the groom, wouldn't be carrying my bride over the threshold. Instead, I ask, 'Do you want the front seat or the back?' After picking the back seat, Shelly quickly falls asleep while I sprawl out, tucking my head under the steering wheel, trying to get comfortable. A few hours later we wake to daylight, walk into the rest stop restrooms, splash some water on our face and brush our teeth. Our moment to ride off into the sunset, happily ever after, has come and gone as we hop back into the car and continue on our journey, assuming things can only get better from here. Twenty-one years later, we're thankful for our first lesson in faithfulness; we were in it to the finish.

Faithful To Do What We're Called To Do

'If you are faithful in little things, you will be faithful in large ones.' - Jesus (Luke 16:10). When following Jesus, he will lead you down the path of faithfulness.

Faithfulness is sticking with it, all the way to the end. It's needed when the inspiration fades and the perspiration begins. Faithfulness is an afterthought in the 'feel good' moment; when the holy goose bumps are a mile high. When they disappear, and the only bumps you have are the bumps and bruises from following Jesus, that's when faithfulness is vital. Receiving eternal life requires faith (Ephesians 2:8, 2 Timothy 4:7), but living the life God is calling you to requires faithfulness.

The Apostle Paul, who we earlier read about, had an encounter with Christ that changed his life. He had a moment of faith, and his life did a one-eighty. He went from being a religious zealot to radical evangelist because he had begun a relationship with the risen Christ. That was just the beginning of what God wanted to accomplish in him and through him. Everything else God desired to do would require that Paul remain faithful.

Nearing the end of his life, Paul writes, *'As for me, my life has already been poured out as an offering to God. The time of my death is near. I have fought the good fight, I have finished the race, and I have remained faithful. And now the prize awaits me-the crown of righteousness, which the Lord, the righteous Judge, will give me on the day of his return. And the prize is not just for me but for all who eagerly look forward to his appearing.'* (2 Timothy 4:6-8) He poured his life into the work of God as an offering to God. He stayed in the fight, engaging in the daily struggles that came with doing what he was called to do. He finished the race, fulfilling the mission of spreading the good news of Jesus in his lifetime. He then says, 'I have remained faithful.' He stuck with it right to the end. Regardless of the circumstances; the persecution, prison time, abandonment from friends, and the burden of leadership, he remained faithful.

Maybe God makes faithfulness a big deal because he knows it won't be easy, yet it's necessary. Unfortunately, not everyone remains faithful. Knowing that, Jesus taught a very vivid lesson to his disciples in Matthew chapters twenty-four and twenty-five. Coming to him privately, they ask, *'What sign will signal your return and the end of the world?'* (Matthew 24:3) After saying some interest things, he changes focus and has a lot to say about remaining faithful to the very end.

The Measuring Stick
Is Faithfulness

'*Again, the Kingdom of Heaven can be illustrated by the story of a man going on a long trip...*' (Matthew 25:14) A guy goes on a trip and decides to entrust his servants with the responsibility of investing some of his money while he's away. He gives one servant five bags of silver. To another, two bags, and to another, he gives one bag. Jesus says that he divided it in proportion to their abilities. Then, sayonara, he takes off on his trip.

Keep in mind the context of Jesus' teaching. His disciples asked, 'What sign will signal your return and the end of the world?' Jesus isn't giving a seminar on investing in the stock market, making a quick buck in real estate, or in long-term mutual funds; he's teaching us how to invest our life, until the very end.

His story continues, '*The servant who received the five bags of silver began to invest the money and earned five more. The servant with two bags of silver also went to work and earned two more. But the servant who received the one bag of silver dug a hole in the ground and hid the master's money.*' (Matthew 25:16-18) Two of the servants go to work and invest what the man gives them. They have faith that there will be a return. One servant, out of fear of losing what he receives, buries it and does nothing. Which servant or servants would you say most honors their master? If you were the master, how would you feel about the two who doubled their money? How would you feel about the one who buried the money? It's interesting to note that Jesus says the amount they receive is in proportion to their abilities. We all have different strengths and weaknesses. Though we have different personalities, talents, and resources, we're all equally accountable for investing our life - who we are and what we have - into God's purposes for our world.

The trip is over, and the master comes home. Eager to see what the servants did with what he gave them, he calls the first servant in, the one to whom was given five bags of silver, and the servant reports that he's doubled his investment. Verse twenty-one says, *'The master was full of praise. 'Well done, my good and faithful servant. You have been faithful in handling this small amount, so now I will give you many more responsibilities. Let's celebrate together!"* The second servant, who received two bags of silver, comes in and reports that he's also doubled his investment. He hears the same response, 'Well done, my good and faithful servant...' They are each equally praised and rewarded with more responsibilities. It's not a contest about who can perform the best and please their master the most. The measuring stick isn't who brings in the most silver. The measuring stick is faithfulness, doing something with what they've been given.

Then something sad happens. The third servant enters and gives his report. He says, *'Master, I knew you were a harsh man, harvesting crops you didn't plant and gathering crops you didn't cultivate. I was afraid I would lose your money, so I hid it in the earth. Look, here is your money back.'* (Matthew 25:24-25) The master's joy evaporates. After speaking with the first two servants, he has to be thinking, 'This is how it's supposed to be.' Now, he's looking into the eyes of the servant who does nothing more than burying what he's received while doubting his master's goodness. He doesn't even break a sweat for his master.

The master replies by saying that if the servant believes he's so cruel, he would have at least put the money in the bank so that it would have earned a little interest. But the master isn't cruel, and he isn't only looking to double each investment. He's looking for faithfulness. He's seeking servants whom he can trust because they invest what they've been given. He has more responsibility to dole out, and those who are faithful are the ones who qualify.

The Man Eating Dog - Remaining Faithful In The Midst Of Failure

The enemy of faithfulness is fear. Servant number three feared failure. Believing his master to be cruel, he despaired over the thought of letting him down. Being faithful is being confident that God is good, not cruel. He's gone through incredible means to show us the depth of his love. Why then would he turn into a merciless taskmaster? It's illogical.

So what do we do when doing what God wants us to do seems to fail? If you'll remember, living by faith is trusting that God is who he says he is, and trying to do what he tells us to do. The failure lies not in the results, but in the effort. To try once takes faith. To try again takes faithfulness.

I'll never forget the day my faith almost got me killed. Trying to be the caring Pastor, I went old school by making some house calls. Standing in front of a big two-story home with a long wrap-around porch, I can't see the front door from the sidewalk but assume it's on the side of the house. A compassionate soul who wants to make a difference in the world, I run up the front steps, and that's when things take a turn for the worst.

Hearing a deep growl, out of the corner of my eye, I see something move; it's a chain. Not the kind of chain you'd use on a Chihuahua, it's a thick, heavy-duty chain - the likes of which you'd use when pulling a snowmobile out of a wintery ditch with a pickup truck. My heart rate is spiking, and my feet freeze with fear, I don't know what to do. 'If I turn and run,' I think, 'he might attack. If I stand still, he might attack.' With few options (true story) I begin quoting Genesis 1:28, where God tells Adam, '*Be fruitful and multiply. Fill the earth and govern it. Reign over the fish in the sea, the birds in the sky, and all the animals that scurry along the ground.*' In an attempt to convince myself that God has given me dominion over fish, birds, and man-eating dogs, I muster up the faith and courage to take baby

152 | *NOW WHAT?*

steps and turn the corner to face the beast attached to the end of the chain.

There he is; the meanest, ugliest, most vicious dog I'd ever seen. He looks like he weighs two hundred pounds, with teeth that seem to hang like fangs and drool that I imagine he uses to wash down the flesh of past victims. The eyes of man meet the eyes of dog. He continues growling while I keep quoting God's Word. Creeping ever so slowly toward the door, with trepidation, I reach over Satan's personal pet, extending my finger for the doorbell, and that's when everything goes blank.

In the blink of an eye, with a bark that rattles my bones, he lunges at me with fierceness unlike I'd ever seen. Not remembering when I turned and ran, or how I got off the porch and past the sidewalk, there I am, standing in the middle of the street. Tipping on cardiac arrest looking for signs that I'd entered the pearly gates, I distinctly hear the voice of a lady down the street yelling, 'I wouldn't go up there if I were you.' 'Thanks, lady. Couldn't you have said something sooner?', is all I can think to say. Publicly humiliated, scared to death, and probably a little wet in the pants, at least I'd live another day to try again - for Jesus, of course.

The Joy Of Faithfulness

Do you remember our look into Joseph's life? Between you and what God's calling you to do is resistance. Always there, its presence doesn't mean that God is absent. He's right there with you. Expect him to do great things, but don't be surprised when you're facing difficulty. Again, James 1:2-4 speaks to this when it says, *'Consider it pure joy, my brothers, whenever you face trials of many kinds, because you know that the testing of your faith develops perseverance. Perseverance must finish its work so that you may be mature and complete, not lacking anything.'*

Often just a test, trials can lead you to believe you're not good enough, smart enough, or talented enough to pull it off. They whisper things like, 'See, I told you. You're in over your head.' Or, 'You missed God, this time, didn't you?' It's in those moments; when failure seems inevitable, that your faith is put to the test. That's when God says, 'Consider it pure joy...' Why? You consider it joy because the testing of your faith is developing perseverance. What is persevering faith? Faithfulness!

Consider it pure joy when living a life surrendered to Christ is harder than you thought it'd be. Consider it pure joy when your obedience to God limits the options and creates difficulty. Consider it pure joy when serving others is inconvenient and goes unappreciated. Consider it pure joy when sacrificing for the Kingdom of God costs you dearly. Consider it pure joy when you follow Jesus as he leads you down this path. It's the back roads and bumpy trails of participation in God's purposes for the world. It's the trail that's been blazed by the heroes of the faith, including Joseph, Job, John the Baptist, and Paul the Apostle. Now, it's your turn and my turn. It's the same for all who call him Leader and Lord, who believe he told the truth when saying, *'Whoever wants to be my disciple must deny themselves and take up their cross and follow me. For whoever wants to save their life will lose it, but whoever loses their life for me will find it.'* (Matthew 16:24-25 NIV)

You may not remember the eggs - over easy, the burnt coffee, the wheat toast or jelly, but do you remember the question he asked? 'When God does something in your life, does he just do it or do we have anything to do with it?' It's our choice to follow him down the path of The Five Essentials: surrender, obedience, service, and sacrifice, remaining faithful to it all and through it all. Yes, we have a lot to do with it. However, there's something God does in our life that only he can do. It's the culmination of his work in us, the reward of our faithfulness and the goal in which God had in mind from the very beginning. Are you ready? You've come this far. It's time to cross the finish line.

CHAPTER FOURTEEN

Be Faithful, Become Fruitful

The Resurrected Orange Tree

I THOUGHT SHE WAS CRAZY, BUT WHAT do I know about orange trees? Growing up in the Midwest, oranges are things that come in bags from the grocery store, or in cartons as juice, not as living, breathing produce hanging on a tree in your back yard. Living in California, orange trees are a regular part of life. What's abnormal is the drought we've been in, a severe drought. Our first two years living in the Golden State, it rained just three or four times. We're beginning to see some relief, but it gets scary when everything is drying up, including the lakes and reservoirs. At one point, we were placed under strict water restrictions. Told not to wash our cars, water the lawn, or spend ex-

155

tra time in the shower, water had become a precious resource, and I became acutely aware of how much I was using. For fear of wasting it, I wouldn't let the water run while brushing my teeth. I'd get just what I needed, then turn it off. It became a personal challenge to see how little water I could use. I began wondering if we were becoming a sequel to The Dust Bowl of the 1930's.

In our back yard stands a lonely little orange tree, alone because it has no brothers or sisters and little because it's supposed to be. What's not intended to be is how sickly our little tree had become. Pale in color and producing only a tiny crop of anemic oranges the year before, the tree seemed destined to give up its ghost and become kindling for the campfire.

One day, Shelly took on the mission of saving this little orange tree. Without violating the water restriction, in a creative spark, she has an idea. Taking an empty plastic ice cream container, while filling up the sink to wash the pots and pans, Shelly first fills up that bucket with water while waiting for it to heat up. She then takes the liquid life outdoors and pours it on the base of our little orange tree. Thinking she's crazy, while laughing, I tell her it's a lost cause. She doesn't care what I say; she has her sights set on saving this tree. I guess she's become a real California tree hugger.

Throwing out my darts of ridicule and sarcasm, one thing I don't do is pay attention to the tree. Then, one day, I see some full-sized oranges sitting on the kitchen counter. 'Did these come off the tree?', I ask. 'Yes,' she says, with the cunning smile of a wife who'd won. Certain they will taste horrible, I peel one and take a bite. I can't believe it. It's the best orange I've ever had. Almost in disbelief, I think I'd just sank my teeth into something straight from the garden of Eden. Speechless, I have to own my loss and praise Shelly for her wisdom, patience, and the great idea of resurrecting the dying little orange tree.

I can no longer buy oranges at the store. Spoiled, I wait for our little tree to produce its fruit. Guess who now collects the excess water from the faucet and pours it at the base of the tree? That's right; she taught me well.

Destined To Be Fruitful

'When you produce much fruit, you are my true disciples. This brings great glory to my Father.' (John 15:8) Oranges are especially juicy and delicious when nurtured with love and picked fresh off the tree, five feet from your backdoor. However, they're nothing like the fruit God produces in your life as you go down the path he calls you to.

Describing our relationship with him, in John 15, Jesus paints the picture of a vine having branches that are producing an abundance of fruit. He is the vine, we're the branches, and God, the Father, is the gardener. As we abide or remain in close relationship with Jesus, God does the work of removing what's undesirable and unhealthy in us to make way for our intended purpose; being fruitful. Much of abiding in Christ is walking the path he leads us down. But what's this fruit Jesus is speaking of? Is it a generic way to describe how God impacts our life, a broad attempt at saying the good stuff comes from him? Is this fruit the elimination of credit card debt? Is it for marriages to be free of strife and filled with love? Is it to stay steady on the emotional rollercoaster called parenting? Is this fruit that of living with less stress, having stronger relationships, and being more fulfilled? God's Word has much to say about all of this but is that the fruit he's referring to when saying in John 15:8, *'When you produce much fruit, you are my true disciples. This brings great glory to my Father.'* What is this evidence, this fruit, of the 'true disciples' of Jesus, that which brings glory to God? Being fulfilled, having a healthy family, and living debt free might honor God, but what if all of that, and much more, is a by-product of this fruit God wants to produce in your life?

Galatians 5:22 describes some of this fruit when it says, *'But the Holy Spirit produces this kind of fruit in our lives: love, joy, peace, patience, kindness, goodness, faithfulness, gentleness, and self-control. There is no law against these things!'* Stop! Did you catch that? No matter how many times you may have read that, heard that, or wondered why you're not experiencing more of that, this stuff is for real! As you remain faithful, God does the work of making you fruitful. Commit to the life he calls you to, and he commits to producing this kind of life in you. Imagine being the one full of it. Love - having a sincere affection for those around you. Joy - being genuinely delighted about life. Peace - experiencing an inner serenity that remains strong, regardless of the circumstances. Patience - the persistence to persevere through thick and thin. Kindness - a friendliness that's fueled by compassion and empathy. Goodness - being someone who's naturally upright and honest. Faithfulness - the one known to be a committed and loyal finisher. Gentleness - someone who doesn't need to force his or her way through life but cooperates with God's process. And, self-control - one who's able to practice restraint in life's most crucial moments. That's the life, the fruit; God desires to create, to produce in your life. Add to that the forgiveness of sin, friendship with God, and life empowered by the Spirit. Regardless of who you are, where you come from, or what you've done, if your life is full of this, you can honestly say, 'Jesus has changed my life.'

Paul, the Apostle, would often pray for others who, like him, were following Jesus. He'd pray that God would help them be attuned to his will and understand the ways in which he works. After praying one such prayer, Paul writes in Colossians 1:10, *'Then the way you live will always honor and please the Lord, and your lives will produce every kind of good fruit. All the while, you will grow as you learn to know God better and better.'* Encouraging even others in much the same way, he writes in Philippians 1:11, *'May you always be filled with the fruit of your salvation-the righteous character produced in your life by Jesus Christ-for this will bring much glory and praise to God.'*

He's the vine, you're the branch, and God is the gardener. The process of pruning is constant as the Holy Spirit produces that which you and everyone who's a part of your life get to enjoy; fruit, fruit, and more fruit.

The secret to living this life is no secret at all. Jesus makes it incredibly clear when he says, *'Remain in me, and I will remain in you. For a branch cannot produce fruit if it is severed from the vine, and you cannot be fruitful unless you remain in me. Yes, I am the vine; you are the branches. Those who remain in me, and I in them, will produce much fruit. For apart from me you can do nothing.'* (John 15:4-5)

The way to the fruitful life isn't classified information, but it is sometimes a struggle. We don't strive or strain to create the virtues of joy and peace, etc. That's because fruit happens; it's the natural by-product of abiding in Christ, of staying close through time spent with him while living a life of surrender, obedience, service, sacrifice, and faithfulness. The battle lies in fighting against the gravitational pull away from these things. It's normal, even natural to want to take control of your life, disobey and disregard God, to look out only for yourself and those in your household, and to consume on yourself all that comes your way. Though it takes an effort to abide, the reward is enormous. Psalm 1:2-3 says, *'But they delight in the law of the Lord, meditating on it day and night. They are like trees planted along the riverbank, bearing fruit each season. Their leaves never wither, and they prosper in all they do.'* In every season and every situation, you are called to abide in Christ, to walk the path he leads you down, and to bear fruit. When you do, God gets the glory, you experience a richer life, and you make this world a better place.

Stop Wondering, Stop Wandering, And Start Living

Thank you. In the uncounted hours I've spent working, and at times, agonizing over how to share in words what God has taught me through my trials, I kept praying that he'd use this book to help someone. If that someone is you, all the work it took to get this in your hands was worth it. I encourage, even challenge you to do two things. First, put into practice what you've just read. If you do, I guarantee that God will change your life. I learned this stuff through living it during a season of life I'll never forget. Understanding these things and applying them saved me from becoming a statistic. That's why I'm confident God can do the same for you.

You no longer need to spend time wandering through life while wondering what God is doing or how he works. You know that when God does something in your life, you have a lot to do with it. You know the path Jesus leads you down as you follow him. You know that losing isn't failure when it comes to living out your faith. You're trusting God enough to try and do what he's calling you to do. Just like Joseph, Job, John the Baptist, and Paul the Apostle, God is doing his greatest work in you during your greatest trials. You're now pursuing a life of surrender, obedience, service, and sacrifice - fearlessly convinced that faithfully sticking with it, you'll experience the fruit that God loves to produce in your life.

Second, don't keep this to yourself. As God leads you down this path and through these things, share it with others. Maybe someday, you'll be sitting across the table from someone, sipping burnt coffee as they ask, 'When God does something in your life, does he just do it or do we have anything to do with it?' Without hesitation, you'll be able to say, 'We do have something to do with it. Let me show you the path that Jesus leads you down when you choose to follow him.' You'll begin by taking them to Matthew 16:24-25, which says, *'Then Jesus said to his disciples, 'Whoever wants to be my disciple must deny themselves and take up their cross and follow me. For whoever wants to save their life will lose it, but whoever loses their life for me will find it.''* (NIV)

ABOUT THE AUTHOR

Scott Rodgers is a pastor, communicator, and consultant to organizational leaders on strategy, culture, and team development. Engaging audiences with humor, energy, and simplicity, Scott's passion is to inspire others to live a life surrendered to Christ. Scott and his wife, Shelly, live near Sacramento, California and have three children.

HOW TO SPREAD THE WORD

To contact the author, place bulk orders, or share 'Now What?' with a friend, go to:

WWW.READNOWWHAT.COM